HERB
GARDENS
& TEA

2006/7

Compiled by
Barty Phillips

•

Published in 2006 by
Margaretta Publishing
PO Box 51752
London NW1 9RU
info@svillas.demon.co.uk

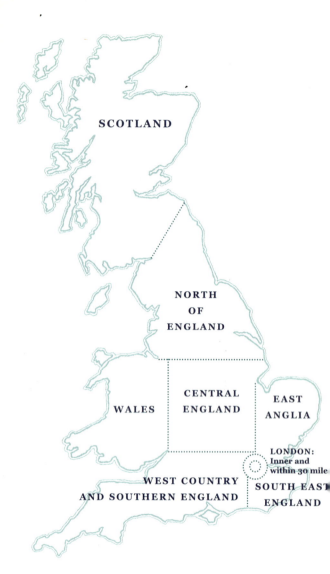

SCOTLAND

NORTH
OF
ENGLAND

WALES

CENTRAL
ENGLAND

EAST
ANGLIA

LONDON:
Inner and
within 30 mile

WEST COUNTRY
AND SOUTHERN ENGLAND

SOUTH EAST
ENGLAND

The Maps

The map above shows the areas covered by
this guide. Each section has an enlarged
map of the area with individual gardens
pinpointed and named.

CONTENTS

3

Introduction

This small book offers a guide to over 100 gardens in England, Scotland and Wales which concentrate largely on herbs. Herb gardens have a unique quality provided by their scents and colours and the knowledge that the herbs they grow have been providing humankind with medicines, culinary delights, household products, cosmetics and other essential ingredients for a civilised and healthy life for many thousands of years.

Today's herb gardens range from the simplest 'cartwheel' culinary beds with herbs growing through the 'spokes', to re-created medieval and cloister gardens, large botanic gardens and an enormous range of gardens large and small, formal and informal, clipped and unkempt. Herb gardens may be enjoyed purely for their peaceful environment or used as sources of plant material for use or for research and as places to study the plants themselves or their history. Some included here are purely herb gardens; others are herb gardens within larger gardens. Several have only recently been created.

Herbs have been affectionately described as 'rugged, helpful little characters'. But the word herb covers an extraordinary number of plants from tiny creeping thymes, through shrubby lavenders and rosemaries to trees such as witch hazel and even the mighty yew, from which a substance called taxol is extracted which is used to combat breast and other cancers. This wonderful variety lends itself to innumerable and varied designs when it comes to gardens. As well as the pleasing and fascinating re-created gardens from the past, emulating the original Paradise Garden with clipped box and yew, straight lines and central sundials or fountains, the present tendency to remember the needs of wildlife relies greatly on herbal plants; wild flower meadows are largely filled with herbs.

The actions of herbs are not bland. On the contrary at Kew the herb garden includes an area of 'poisonous plants' and at Alnwick the Poison Garden is a fascinating feature. A number of highly poisonous plants are used medicinally. Many of the gardens featured in this booklet are well labelled with descriptions of each plant and its uses. Others are part of demonstration gardens of small specialist nurseries, where the staff can give valuable advice on growing and harvesting herbs. Yet others are gardens purely for enjoyment, with seats and arbours from which to savour the heady herbal scents and to watch the bees and butterflies. In one garden I visited, a peahen was quietly sitting on her eggs under a small bay tree.

Visiting gardens can be quite thirsty work, so for each garden I have suggested places where you can get a refreshing cup of tea, if not in the garden itself, then quite nearby. Where possible the tea-shops have an interesting menu and pleasant settings with good views – many of them offer herbal as well as other specialist varieties of tea and, if you're lucky, you may get freshly baked herbal scones and cakes.

Barty Phillips
2005

NB. It is recommended that you contact the gardens before your visit to check opening dates and times.

LONDON: INNER

- Knebworth House

A 1 M

HATFIELD ● Hatfield House

Chenies Manor
●

M 25

ENFIELD ● ● Capel Manor

● AMERSHAM

HACKNEY

● Geffrye Museum

London Zoo ●
WESTMINSTER Tradescant Gdn

Kew ● ●
Chelsea Physic Gdn
Fulham Palace Gdn

M 25

● Wisley

A 3

The sites of the gardens shown on this map are approximate. They will give an indication as to how you might plan your visits. For precise instructions on finding the gardens, please refer to the specific information for each garden.

Chelsea Physic Garden

66 Royal Hospital Road, London SW14 4HS
Tel 020 7352 5646   www.chelseaphysicgarden.co.uk

*2 miles from Piccadilly Circus; tube: Sloane Square; bus
239 from Victoria. Entrance on Swan Walk on public days*

Open Apr to Oct, Wed 12–5; Sun 2–6; special openings for
the snowdrops in Feb and during Chelsea Flower Show
week
Admission charge. Wheelchair access
Shop; plants for sale
Owner Trustees of Chelsea Physic Garden

THE HERB GARDEN

This 4 acre garden on the banks of the Thames is the
second oldest botanic garden in the UK, founded by
the Society of Apothecaries in 1673 as a place for
apprentices to learn to identify medicinal plants. It is
a truly secret garden entered through tall walls via a
small door. During the eighteenth century it became
an important botanic garden and still grows around
5000 medicinal plants and those of ethnobotanic
interest as well as plants named or introduced by
people associated with garden history. The mild
microclimate created by tall red brick walls, its
south-facing aspect and the shelter of the city enable
many tender plants to be grown. There are large,
historic trees including a male and female *Ginkgo
biloba*, a cork oak (*Quercus suber*) and a productive
olive (*Olea europaea*). This is still a working physic
garden, involved in scientific research, plant
conservation and education. A walk round its wide
paths and categorised beds at any time of year offers
all sorts of pleasures and in the tradition of botanic
gardens, the labelling is informative. Particular
points of interest are the **Pharmaceutical Garden**
displaying plants that yield therapeutic compounds
of proven value in current medicinal practice and are
in world-wide use today including the Madagascar
periwinkle (*Catharanthus roseus*) used in anti-

cancer drugs, woolly foxglove (*Digitalis lanata*)
which contains digoxin, used to prevent abnormal
heart rhythms, meadowsweet (*Filipendula ulmaria*)
the plant from which salicylic acid was first made in
1835 leading to the introduction of aspirin in 1899.
The Perfume and Aromatherapy Borders
contain plants which yield oils such as lemon
verbena (*Aloysia triphylla*), rosemary, lavender,
Rosa centifolia, *Pelargonium odoratissimum* and
Iris germanica var. *florentina*. Other displays
include culinary herbs, edible flowers, poisonous
plants and dye plants.

TEA

Teas are available on public open days and include a
choice of herbal teas, cakes and scones in a spacious
hall with pretty tablecloths and fresh flowers.

Fulham Palace Herb Garden

Fulham Palace Road, Hammersmith, London SW6
Tel 020 7736 9820

*Tube: Putney Bridge; buses: 74, 220, 430 to Fulham
Palace Road then 5 minute walk; 14, 141, 22, 85, 93, 265
to Putney Bridge then 10 minute walk. There is metered
parking in Bishop's Avenue*

Open botanic and herb garden daily all day (Museum open
Sat and Sun 2–5).
Admission free. Wheelchair access to botanic garden,
partial access to herb garden
Garden and museum
Owner Leased by London Borough of Hammersmith

THE HERB GARDEN

The old Bishop's Palace at Fulham is now council
offices but there are 13 acres of garden and a
fascinating small museum. The garden first became
famous in the seventeenth century when Bishop
Compton imported rare species of plants including
magnolia and was the first person to grow them in

Europe. None of his original plants survive but there are grand specimen trees including a giant oak from 1550; you can also spy, amongst others, a catalpa, cedar of Lebanon, copper beech, tulip tree, cercis, and weeping limes. Within the old walled garden is a magical not-quite-wilderness, pretty overgrown with avenues of apple trees and beech hedges creating mysterious spaces. It is in many ways a true secret garden waiting to be discovered and renovated. Within this space a herb knot garden was planted by Hammersmith and Fulham Council in the early 1980s with botanic beds and a wisteria pergola. It takes the form of a series of 'family' beds such as the umbelliferae (angelica, caraway, coriander, fennel, dill), the mints (thyme, lemon balm, hyssop, rosemary, basil), the cruciferae (wallflower, candytuft, honesty) and others. This garden is waiting for serious renovation, its box hedges are a little unkempt and the soil and plants need renewing. Nevertheless, it is a pleasure to visit, with its Tudor archway and abundance of blackberries in August. An information board by the gate shows a plan of the garden and where each herb is grown.

TEA

There's no tea-room on site but in Bishop's Park, opposite, you'll find Jackie's Cottage Café selling basic tea and coffee with a choice of 5 herbal teas plus sandwiches and the kind of baked beans/baked potatoes/crisps menu children love. Enjoy it under maple trees beside raised beds of busy Lizzies and a wisteria pergola. Rather more sophisticated is Tinto Coffee, 117 Fulham Palace Road just across the road from the Fulham Palace Garden Centre, decorated in a contemporary style with outdoor seating for sunny days and a patio heater for cold ones. It specialises in freshly ground coffee but also serves various teas including iced tea, spiced tea, green tea and various cakes and pastries. It is friendly to children and dogs. Open Mon to Sun 7–9. Tel 020 7731 1420. Otherwise

there are several cafés to choose from near Putney
Bridge tube station.

Geffrye Museum Herb Garden

Geffrye Museum, Kingsland Road, London E2 8EA
Tel 020 7739 9893   www.geffrye-museum.org.uk

*Buses: 67, 149, 242, 243, 394; underground: Liverpool
Street then buses 149 or 242 from Bishopsgate; Old Street
(exit 2) 15 min walk or bus 243.*

Open Museum: Tue to Sat 10–5; Sun and bank holidays
12–5; closed Mon (except bank holidays), 1 Jan, Good
Friday, 24, 25, 26 Dec; Gardens open 1 Apr to 31 Oct
Admission free. Wheelchair access
Shop
Owner Geffrye Museum Trust

THE HERB GARDEN

The Geffrye is the only museum in the UK to
specialise in period interiors of the urban middle
classes from 1600 to the present day. Set in elegant
eighteenth-century buildings it is backed by an
award winning walled herb garden which contains
over 170 different herbs. Twelve beds each contain
informal groupings of herbs which share a common
use, so there are beds for cosmetic, medical, culinary,
household, aromatic and dye plants. In addition to
the Herb garden there is a series of spaces that
reflect the period domestic interiors within the
museum, including a Tudor Knot Garden. The Late
Elizabethan Garden (1550–1620) reflects the modest
gardens of town houses of the period, providing
culinary, medicinal and household herbs, pot herbs
(vegetables) and flowers in geometric, raised beds.
The Mid-Late Georgian Garden (1760–1800) shows
the garden as an extension of the house, featuring
simplicity and tidiness with paved or rolled gravel
paths, geometric beds, box edging and clipped
evergreens. The Mid-Late Victorian Garden

(1860–1890) reflects the Victorian passion for gardening and plant collecting. The Edwardian Garden (1900–1914) shows increasingly informal plantings inspired by cottage gardens and an interest in medieval plants.

TEA

The light, contemporary restaurant building overlooks the gardens. Here you can get cream teas, home-cooked meals and light snacks. To book a table in advance call 020 7739 9893.

Kew Herb Garden

Royal Botanic Gardens, Kew, Richmond, Surrey TW9 3AB
Tel 020 8332 5655   www.rgbkew.org.uk

On the south bank of the Thames 6 miles SW of London. Bus: 61; rail and tube: Kew Gardens; rail: Kew Bridge

Open daily except Christmas Eve and Christmas Day; opening times vary, please ring for details
Admission charge. Most of garden suitable for wheelchairs
Gardens; shop
Owner Trustees of the Royal Botanic Gardens

THE HERB GARDEN

Kew has a long history involving the royal house of Hanover in the eighteenth century. It has all manner of fascinating aspects from ancient trees, fantastic glasshouses, woodlands, wild areas, temples, a pagoda and so much more. The Palm House contains orchids (Kew has the oldest known collection of living orchids), including the vanilla orchid as well as rubber trees. The Order Beds and Rose Pergola were introduced by Sir Joseph Hooker in the nineteenth century as a learning library of flowering plants for students of botany and horticulture. The plants were systematically arranged, as in most botanic gardens, so they could be easily located for study. The Rock Garden has alpine plants, Mediterranean plants and those that come from similar climate areas such as

Admission free, donations welcome
Shop; library; exhibitions
Owner The Museum of Garden History

THE HERB GARDEN

The Museum of Garden History was founded in 1977 at the former church of St Mary-at-Lambeth next to Lambeth Palace. It is named after the John Tradescants, father and son, seventeenth-century gardeners to royalty and the aristocracy and successful plant hunters during the seventeenth century (whose tombs are in the Churchyard). Inside the building is a fascinating collection of gardening artefacts, temporary exhibitions and a small library. A small formal garden has been created in part of the churchyard reached through the museum. It is a garden full of peace and interest with a knot garden designed by Lady Salisbury whose family first employed John Tradescant the elder at Hatfield House. This garden is in the style of those at Hatfield designed by Tradescant. The garden is edged with box; cotton lavender has been used for the T (for Tradescant) shapes that divide the beds. Other herbs have been donated from all over the country. The Museum has used mainly plants known to have grown in Britain during the seventeenth century including some introduced by the Tradescants themselves.

TEA

The Courtyard Café within the museum offers tea, coffee, cold drinks and delicious home-made light lunches. These can be enjoyed in the café itself or sitting peacefully in the garden among its historic tombstones and other links to the past.

Westminster Abbey College Garden

The Chapter Office, 20 Dean's Yard, St James's Park,
Westminster, London SW1P 3PA
Tel 020 7222 5152   www.westminster-abbey.org

*Next to Parliament square, opposite the Houses of
Parliament. 500m from Westminster tube. Buses: 3, 11, 53,
77A, 88, 159*

Open winter 10–4, summer 10-6, Tue, Wed, Thur.
Donations invited. Wheelchair access
Owner The Dean and Chapter

THE HERB GARDEN

Westminster Abbey is a working religious abbey and
is closed on Sundays. The College Garden is on a site
that has been in continuous cultivation for more than
900 years. The Abbey's first infirmary garden was
established here in the eleventh century. The
Infirmarer, a Senior Monk of the Abbey, had care of
the sick and elderly members of the community and
dispensed medicines for local people. He would have
directed the planting and cultivation of the various
herbs needed for medicinal purposes. The area is
now occupied by a knot garden, its spaces filled with
white and blue lavender. In the three borders to the
side a selection of medicinal herbs has been planted
with another dozen or so arranged among them in
pots. Records kept in the Abbey Library mention the
construction of a herbarium which was completed in
1306. The oldest living things in the present garden
are the five tall plane trees *Platanus x hispanicus*,
planted in 1850. Due to the high lead content of the
soil many of the herbs growing in the garden today
cannot be used for medicinal purposes. The Garth,
the Little Cloister Garden and St Catherine's Garden
are not generally open to the public but may be
viewed when the College Garden is open.

TEA

There are self-service cafés in the cloister and outdoors. Or you could get a sophisticated full afternoon tea in opulent surroundings at the famous Savoy Hotel in the Strand. It is advisable to book, especially at weekends. Tel 020 7836 4343.

30 MILES ROUND LONDON

Capel Manor

Capel Manor College, Bullsmoor Lane, Enfield, Middx EN1 4RQ
Tel 020 83664442   www.capel.ac.uk

Just off the A10 by Junction 25 of M25

Open Mar to Oct daily 10–6 (or dusk if sooner); Nov to Feb Wed only
Admission charge. Wheelchair access
Gift shop; bookshop; workshops; lectures; garden walks
Owner Capel Manor Corporation

Capel Manor is run as a college for horticulture, garden design and related skills whose gardens provide an invaluable resource for students to put into practice what they learn. The fascinating collection of gardens is open to the public. There are three main areas: the older gardens surrounding the eighteenth-century house with an Italianate holly maze, a woodland section, interesting mature trees, lawns, ponds, knots and a walled garden; the National Gardening Centre made up of an interesting – if rather higgledy piggledy – collection of small themed gardens offering numerous ideas for modern gardeners; a section of the grounds run by *Gardening Which?* for trials and experiments with more small gardens, including a garden for drought and a herb garden.

THE HERB GARDEN

The gardens are changing and developing all the time. Some are specifically herb gardens, many rely largely on herbs for their interest. There is a Low Allergen Garden designed by Lucy Huntington, a Wildflower Garden with a pool and silver birches and the scent of wild garlic, and a Slate Garden made of Welsh slate with raised herb beds. An avenue of pleached lime trees border these gardens. A separate area includes a Feast of the Senses Garden designed for partially sighted and blind people with different sounds of water and many different scents. It is worth taking time to wander and inspect because there are many gardens and plenty of food for herbal thought.

TEA

The restaurant has a somewhat 'canteeny' ambience but you can get tea, herbal teabags and cakes, scones and biscuits here.

Chenies Manor

Chenies, Rickmansworth, Bucks WD3 6ER
Tel 01494 762888

4 miles E of Rickmansworth on A404 in the centre of Chenies village

Open Apr to Oct Wed and Thur 2–5 and Bank Holiday Mon
Admission charge. Wheelchair access
Owners Mrs A Macleod Matthews

THE HERB GARDEN

This early Tudor brick house sits in the middle of a series of beautifully kept gardens intended to be viewed from various rooms in the house and to furnish inward vistas of the buildings, very much in the Tudor style. Through a green and white garden and beyond a ha-ha is an enormous formal grass parterre with a 1000-year old oak tree, many clipped yews and urns and an award-winning yew maze planted in 1991. You enter the walled Physic Garden through other gardens where Henry VIII spent time with Anne Boleyn and Katherine Howard. There is a sunken garden full of colour, an avenue of hooped arches covered with clematis and vines, herbaceous borders and much more to delight and please. A small door leads down steep steps into the Physic Garden, a recent creation of Elizabeth Macleod Matthews which reflects an almost universal practice in late medieval homes of any size – a collection of herbs with medicinal properties, real or supposed, and others with power to scent or dye or flavour food. This garden is made up of six plots. The central bed contains a stone fountain in the middle of cotton lavender and verbascum and four beds with grass paths. There is a poison bed, beds of dye plants and others of medicinal and culinary herbs. Everything is well labelled with detailed descriptions of the plants and uses of herbs in the past.

TEA

A choice of teas including herbal teas accompanied by delicious home-made cakes made by the local WI among others are available in a pretty barn where you can sit indoors or outside under apple trees and clipped bay.

Hatfield House Herb Gardens

Hatfield, Hertfordshire AL9 5NQ
Tel 01707 262832   www.hatfield-house.co.uk

In the centre of Hatfield, 20 miles N of London, Junction 3 of A1(M)

Open Apr to end Sep, Sat to Wed, 11–5.30. East gardens open only on Mon (except bank holidays). Whenever special events take place, the park, house and gardens may not be open. Please check first

Admission charge. Wheelchair access
Gift shop; restaurant
Owner Marquess of Salisbury

THE HERB GARDEN

The stately Jacobean house was built in pink brick by Robert Cecil in 1607 and the family has owned it ever since. The garden (English Heritage Grade 1) was originally designed by John Tradescant the Elder. Over 25 years the Dowager Lady Salisbury worked on the garden to extraordinary effect and it is now one of the finest organic gardens in the country. The knot garden in front of the Old Palace is surrounded by high grassy banks full of wild flowers, primroses, cowslips and other tiny flowers. The West Garden is made up of many different spaces. There is a privy garden, a scented garden and a large and important herb garden designed in 1975 which is full of scented and useful plants. It has four main paths leading to a centrally placed sundial. The paths are stone flags with an apple-scented path down the centre planted with chamomile 'Treneague'. There are chamomile seats surrounded by thymes, lavenders and sages. It has four large beds leading to eight circular plots encircling the sundial. Herbs include foxglove, rosemary, bronze and green fennel, old-fashioned roses, thyme, hyssop and marjoram. Annual herbs are mixed with perennials and include borage, chervil, pot marigold and basil. The whole is surrounded by sweetbriar roses, clipped to a height of 60cm, and standard scented honeysuckles mark the entrances to the inner circle.

TEA

The restaurant is in the cluster of old stable buildings that also house the toilets and shop. Here you can get afternoon tea with scones and cakes as well as snacks and hot lunches.

The Jekyll Herb Garden at Knebworth

Knebworth House, Knebworth, Herts SG3 6PY
Tel 01438 812661   www.knebworthhouse.com

28 miles N of London; Junction 7 of the A1(M)

Open Mar to Aug weekends and bank holidays; weekday
opening dates and times vary, please check first
Gardens, shop, restaurant
Owner The Hon Henry Lytton Cobbold

This Tudor mansion has been the home of the Lytton
family since 1490. There have been gardens here
since the 1600s. The present layout dates from
Victorian and Edwardian times. The central formal
area was simplified by Sir Edwin Lutyens in the early
twentieth century. Since the 1980s much work has
gone into redesigning the garden which is made up
of many different areas. There is a pleached lime
walk, a rose garden, a tall clipped hew hedge with
niches for statuary, a rose garden, a gold garden, a
malus walk and wildflower meadows, a maze
bordered by roses and honeysuckles, two ponds,
wilderness and woodland walks and the Wall Border.

THE HERB GARDEN

Amongst it all sits the Jekyll Herb Garden designed
by Gertrude Jekyll in 1907 and built, according to
her original instructions, in 1982. The design is of
interlacing circles in the form of a 'quincunx' using
red engineering brick (which won't be affected by
frost) for the paths. There is lavender in the middle
bed, rosemary for the circular beds and clipped
rosemary links the spaces between the beds. Chervil
seeds itself all around. The edges of the borders are
filled with golden and variegated herbs. Lavender
and rosemary planted round the garden seats waft
their scents around. York stone paths hold creeping
thymes and chamomile in their crevices and cracks.
The Brick Garden and Pergola, designed by Edwin
Lutyens (who married into the family) has typically

detailed brick paths to his design (rediscovered in 1980) and planted with old roses and blue and grey herbaceous plants. The Walled Garden has been recently designed in a pattern of circles to grow culinary herbs and vegetables.

TEA

The new Garden Terrace Room alongside the barns and conference centre gives views of the rose gardens and borders and serves meals, homemade sandwiches with exotic fillings and traditional teas and homemade cakes.

Wisley Herb Garden

RHS Garden Wisley, Woking, Surrey GU23 6QB
Tel 01483 224234 www.rhs.org

20 miles SW of London and 7 miles N of Guildford on the A3, Junction 10 of the M25

Open all year except Christmas Day, Mon to Fri 10–6 (4.30 Nov to Feb); Sat and Sun 9–6 (4.30 Nov to Feb); opens 9am bank holidays
Admission charge (RHS members, plus one guest, free).
Wheelchair access
Shop, bookshop, plant centre
Owner Royal Horticultural Society

Wisley is the flagship garden of the Royal Horticultural Society and its 240 acres are made up of different areas demonstrating different types of plants and gardens and the best in horticultural and gardening practices. There is an alpine house, a magnificent rock garden, a fruit field a, glasshouse, a series of model gardens illustrating design ideas for small gardens, woodland areas, grasses and much more.

THE HERB GARDEN

The Herb garden, designed by Lucy and Francis Huntington was opened in 2003. It is based on a series of circles in threes. There are three entrances, three outer areas and three central circles around the sundial. On the sundial you can read the proverb 'All the flowers of all the tomorrows are in the seeds of today and yesterday'. The herbs are divided into culinary, cosmetic, insect repellent, medicinal, apothecary, North American and Chinese herbs, herbs for pot-pourri and potentially harmful plants. The beds are divided by brick paths and there are rose arches to give shelter and height.

Rose lovers should not miss the Golden Jubilee Rose Garden, also opened in 2003 displaying a collection of modern roses including hybrid tea, floribunda, English and modern shrub roses, climbers, ramblers, groundcover and patio roses, most introduced over the last 20 years.

TEA

Conservatory Café serves Wisley's famous cakes baked on the premises. Indoor or outdoor seating available, but watch out for greedy little song birds who will steal more than the crumbs if given half a chance. Open 10am weekdays, 9am weekends and bank holidays (also serves drinks, sandwiches, salads, snacks and hot lunches).

Coffee Shop (to the front of the shop) serves a full range of speciality coffees with cakes, snacks and sandwiches. There is also a Terrace Restaurant which offers lunches and Sunday breakfasts.

SOUTH EAST ENGLAND

LONDON

• Hall Place

MAIDSTONE

• Leeds Castle

TONBRIDGE

• Downderry Nursery

Yalding Organic Gdns •   • Iden Croft

• Crown House

Bateman's •   • Sissinghurst

Clinton Lodge •   HAILSHAM

BRIGHTON • • Michelham Priory

Merryweather's Herbs

The sites of the gardens shown on
this map are approximate. They will give
an indication as to how you might plan
your visits. For precise instructions on
finding the gardens, please refer to the
specific information for each garden.

Clinton Lodge

Fletching, Nr Uckfield, E Sussex TN22 3ST
Tel 01825 722952

In main village street

Open by appointment and for NGS
Admission charge. Not suitable for wheelchairs
Plants for sale
Owner Sir Hugh and Lady Collum

Carolean and Georgian house with 6 acre formal and romantic gardens overlooking parkland.

THE HERB GARDEN

There are several gardens, designed over the last 30 years by the present owners with the help of garden designers Diana Baskervyle-Glegg and Jonathan Treyer-Evans. There are yew hedges, a pleached lime walk, a canal garden and an allée of fastigiate hornbeams. There are formal gardens based on different periods, including an Elizabethan style herb garden with chamomile paths and turf seats, a true feast for the senses, a medieval-style potager, a rose allée and a wildflower garden. Of particular interest for the herb lover are the old roses and the double herbaceous borders.

TEA

Teas are provided on NGS days and for booked visits.

Crown House Garden

Sham Farm Road, Eridge Green, Tunbridge Wells, E Sussex TN3 9JU   Tel 01892 864389

5 miles E of Crowborough, 3 miles SW of Tunbridge Wells off A26

Open by appointment May to Oct and for NGS in July
Admission charge
Owner Major L Cave

THE HERB GARDEN

Here are 1½ acres designed as a series of gardens on a gentle slope with panoramic views over the Sussex countryside. The garden is still being developed. Features include a lily pond and a croquet lawn, an arboretum, heather, rose and herb gardens, ending in a paved and scented seating area enclosed by a trellis of roses and sweet peas, surrounding an ornamental pond with a fountain. The herb garden and rose walk lead to a lawn and shrubbery.

TEA

Elegant teas are provided for NGS days and for booked visits.

Downderry Nursery

Pillar Box Lane, Hadlow, Tonbridge TN11 9SW
Tel 01732 810081   www.downderry-nursery.co.uk

Follow tourist signs off A26 NE of Hadlow

Open May to Oct Tue to Sun 10–5
Admission free. Wheelchair access
Shop selling lavender products; nursery
Owner Dr Simon J Charlesworth

THE HERB GARDEN

This exceptional specialist nursery is set in a peaceful old walled garden and has an enormous list of lavenders including very unusual ones. It houses the National Collections of Lavender and Rosemary. You can feast your eyes on colours and fill your head with fragrance to your heart's content. A key feature is the circular lavender maze. Recently Dr Charlesworth has started to distil lavender oils and sell the products. The nursery propagates most of the plants sold. There has been much confusion surrounding the nomenclature of the genus *Lavandula* but the Downderry catalogue clearly defines the different species and lists varieties under the relevant species.

TEA

There is no provision for tea at the nursery but about 6 miles away the Fir Tree House Tea Rooms in Penshurst provides fresh home-made cakes, scones and teabreads in a Tudor, wooden frame building with a cottage garden at the back (Tel 01892 870392).

Hall Place

Bexley Heritage Trust, Bourne Road, Bexley,
Kent DA5 1PQ   Tel 01322 526574

Off the A2 on Bourne Road

Open gardens Feb to Oct 9–dusk; Nov to Jan 9–4.40
Admission free. Wheelchair access
Gift shop; nursery; visitor centre; mansion; museum
Owner Bexley Heritage Trust

Hall Place is a Grade I listed sixteenth-century house with a seventeenth-century extension on the south side. The walled garden (now the nursery) would have supplied much of the 'green' food for the original household. It has been developed as a recreational and educational feature and produces bedding plants for the gardens with exotics such as bananas in the greenhouses. There are rivers and pools with lots of water fowl.

THE HERB GARDEN

There are a number of model gardens and allotments including a Flora-for-Fauna garden actively promoting biodiversity, with only native British plants to provide habitats and food for native wildlife such as birds, butterflies and small mammals. Many ancient yews have interesting topiary trimmed and tied in three times a year. There's a rock garden, heather garden, sunken garden and enclosed garden and, of course, the herb garden which has been specially adapted for the blind with labels in Braille. The rose garden holds 4,000 roses laid out in Tudor style with herbaceous borders.

TEA

The Hall Place Café can provide teas and light refreshments. If you want something more substantial the Jacobean Barn, refurbished in 1990 provides a civilised environment for a Beefeater Restaurant.

Iden Croft Herbs

Frittenden Road, Staplehurst, Kent TN12 0DH
Tel 01580 891432   www.herbs-uk.com

In Staplehurst village, 8 miles S of Maidstone by A229

Open all year Mon to Sat and bank holidays; (Mar to Sep 11–5)
Admission charge. Wheelchair access
Nursery and mail order
Owner Philip Haynes

This whole area is only a few feet above sea level in the heart of the Weald of Kent. The garden was created in the 1970s by Rosemary Titterington who grew herbs for wholesale and retail, fresh-cut herbs for the catering trade, edible flowers for special menus and a range of fresh herbs for cosmetics. The new owners are continuing her tradition.

THE HERB GARDEN

Iden Croft sells a vast range of herbs and has excellent ornamental gardens designed to flow into one another and including a Tudor walled garden, herbaceous beds, a garden for the blind, partially sighted or disabled with sitting places to enjoy the scents. The idea is to show how herbs and aromatic plants can be used for colour, scent and practical uses throughout the year. Holds the National Collections of Mentha and Origanum and has large collections of lavender and thymes. A pathway through the garden is made from local Bethesden marble and through its cracks grow many different thymes.

29

TEA

Light refreshments are available in the tea room at Iden Croft. Claris's, 1–3 High Street, Biddenden is just 5 miles away at the junction of the A262 and A274. In a fifteenth-century timber-framed building it offers speciality teas in fine china, cream teas, superb home-made cakes as well as savoury snacks, soup and toasted sandwiches. Open Tue to Sun 10.30–5.30. Tel 01580 291025.

Leeds Castle

Nr Maidstone, Kent ME17 1PL
Tel 01622 765 400   www.leeds-castle.com

4 miles E of Maidstone by A20 and B2163; Junction 8 of M20

Open daily Mar to Oct 10–5; Nov to Feb 10–3
Admission charge. Wheelchair access
Gift shop; plants for sale
Owner Leeds Castle Foundation

Sitting in the middle of the Weald of Kent this romantic castle is surrounded by a moat.

THE HERB GARDEN

The old cutting garden was replaced as the Culpeper Garden by the garden designer Russell Page in 1980. It consists of a series of box-edged beds filled with herbaceous plants and roses. Page's idea was that 'you could walk this way and that through a field of flowers'. The roses tumble over the formal shapes of the box hedges in a most charming and scented ramble. There is also a bed of culinary herbs for use in the castle kitchen. The National Collection of Monarda (bergamot) is held here with five species and 15 cultivars. There is also an effective yew maze with statues and an impressive grotto in honour of Lord Culpeper, a relative of the famous seventeenth-century herbalist Nicholas Culpeper, who owned the castle at that time.

30

TEA

You can have a traditional cream tea in the Jacobean Fairfax Hall, which used to be a tithe barn, where you can enjoy a lakeside terrace view of this wonderful castle.

Merryweather's Herbs

Merryweather's Farm, Chilsham Lane, Herstmonceux, Hailsham, E Sussex BN27 4QH
Tel 01323 831 726   www.morethanjustagarden.co.uk

In Herstmonceux turn into West End (between the Woolpack Inn and Touchstone pine shop). After 1/2 mile turn right into single track Chilsham Lane. Merryweather's is on the right just after a small white bridge.

Open Jun, Jul, Aug Fri to Sun 10–5
Admission charge. Grass paths are not easy for wheelchairs. Nursery
Owner Ian and Liz O'Halloran

The gardens and nursery have been built up within the last eight years. There is a productive kitchen garden, providing food for the household of three which is self-sufficient in vegetables. There is a wildlife pond and the Lizardopolis, a hibernation mound for lizards, slow worms and grass snakes.

THE HERB GARDEN

The herb garden was planted in 2002 where the herbs are grouped in themed beds. In the inner beds are culinary herbs and in the outer beds medicinal, bee and butterfly attractants, dye plants, household plants, Chinese or oriental herbs and plants with animal-related names. The hornbeam hedges, planted in 1998, are now tall enough to provide the intended protection for the garden and retain the scents of the aromatic plants to provide a closed, intimate feeling.

TEA

Merryweather's do not provide teas but Scolfes Tea
Rooms, Boreham Street, Hailsham, less than 5 miles
away, has a variety of teas including herb teas and
home-made cakes and scones. Open 10.30–5 all year
except Mondays. Tel 01323 833296. The Pilgrim's
Rest, 1 High Street, Battle is about 8 miles to the
East. It's in a medieval building and offers a range of
speciality teas in china pots, and fresh cakes made on
site, plus a selection of savoury snacks. Tel 01424
772314.

Michelham Priory

Upper Dicker, Nr Hailsham, E Sussex BN2 3QS
Tel 01323 844 224   www.sussexpast.co.uk

Off A22, 2 miles W of Hailsham

Open daily late Mar to Oct; rest of Mar and Nov Sun only.
Admission charge. Wheelchair access
Gift shop; plants and produce for sale
Owner Sussex Archaeological Society

The moated Priory was built in 1229 but only the
Prior's Room and the tall gate tower by the moat (the
longest medieval water-filled moat in England) still
survive. The spectacular grounds include a
herbaceous border, bog garden, bold waterside
plantings, wilderness walk, lawns and a moat walk.
There is a productive vegetable garden, a cloister, an
orchard, and of course, a reconstructed physic
garden (planted in 1981) set in one of the lawns on
the south side of the house.

THE HERB GARDEN

The gardens employ a rich diversity of styles, some
historic, others more contemporary. The Cloister
Garden combines medieval design and planting to
give a flavour of gradening from the oeriod. The
Physic Garden is based on the plan which

Charlamagne commissioned for the Monastery of St Gall in Switzerland. It contains over ninety plants used in medicine and cooking, many of them grown from seed at the nearby agricultural college and the rest obtained as plants from various herb nurseries, local gardens, allotments and WI markets. The garden is designed to show the plants that might have been used in practical herbal medicine rather than for a study of the subject. All the plants grown here would have been known in England during the sixteenth century and many can be recognized today as plants which grow wild in hedgerows and fields. Plants are arranged in groups according to their medicinal uses. They include lily-of-the-valley (rheumatism), stitchwort, horehound and violet (childbirth and children's diseases); sage, soapwort and tansy (household uses), mallow and calamint and many more. Amusing descriptive labels are engraved on blue enamel and show monks preparing various herbs. Designed by an American art student, Patricia Musick, they add greatly to the character of the garden. Seats invite you to sit and enjoy the peace and history of this garden. The Kitchen Garden is both productive and beautiful with a range of fruit, vegetables and cut flowers throughout the year. It also features a sub-tropical style border in summer and autumn. The Orchard, planted with meadow plantings of long grass and wild flowers, is another peaceful spot.

TEA

There is a good restaurant in the old barn buildings with various teas including Earl Grey and a variety of home-made cakes and other teatime delights plus other food. On a fine day you can take your tea on the expansive lawns under burgeoning growth under green parasols.

Sissinghurst Herb Garden

Sissinghurst Castle, Nr Cranbrook, Kent TN17 2AB
Tel 01580 710700 email: sissinghurst@nationaltrust.org.uk

2 miles NE of Cranbrook, 1 mile E of Sissinghurst Village (A262)

Open late Mar to late Oct, times vary, please phone first. Admission charge (NT members free). Wheelchair access. Shop

Owner The National Trust

THE HERB GARDENS

Vita Sackville-West's great garden, designed as a series of enclosed spaces, is full of herbs wherever you go, from the nuts in the Nuttery to the geometric dividing hedges of yew. The Herb Garden was the last of the separate gardens to be planted and work did not begin until 1938 when it was a modest area with only a dozen or so different herbs. It has since been considerably enlarged with twenty small beds containing many plants cultivated for use in the kitchen and for their decorative foliage. The garden is traditionally designed in the shape of a cross or Paradise garden and surrounded by a high yew hedge. A large marble bowl resting on three lions brought back by the Nicolsons from their travels makes the centrepiece. The famous stone seat was built by a chauffeur. Many of the herbs that feature in Vita's poetry can be seen here including sweet woodruff grown because it was good natured and would grow under trees. Others were rosemary, lavender and dill. The thyme lawn is just beyond the herb garden and is made up of different varieties of thyme.

TEA

There is a licensed restaurant with typical afternoon teas in National Trust wholesome style.

Yalding Organic Gardens

Benover Road, Yalding, Near Maidstone, Kent ME18 6EX
Tel 01622 814650   www.hdra.org.uk

6 miles SW of Maidstone, 1/2 mile S of Yalding village on the B2162

Open May to Sep, Wed to Sun 10–5; Apr, Oct weekends 10–5
Admission charge (HDRA and RHS members free).
Wheelchair access
Shop
Owner Henry Doubleday Research Association (HDRA)

The HDRA (Garden Organic) is Europe's largest organic membership organisation. At Yalding, nestled against a traditional Kentish backdrop of hop gardens and oast houses, there are display gardens showing the best of every aspect of organic gardening. There is a unique combination of a tour through garden history and organic techniques set against a backdrop of beautiful mixed borders. They inspire reflection on mankind's experience of gardening over the centuries.

THE HERB GARDENS

From the Woodland Walk, through the Apothecary's Garden, the Medieval Garden, the Knot Garden, the nineteenth-century Cottager's Garden, the Victorian Artisan's Garden, Edwardian Herbaceous Borders, World War II Dig for Victory Garden and the 1950s Allotment. The Apothecary's Garden holds a host of plants that were used from the thirteenth century onwards for medicinal purposes, in cooking or to mask unpleasant smells, set out as a monastic herb garden with 19 beds. The Medieval Garden is a perfumed flowery mead. Its verdant carpet, spangled with flowers, was a place for lords and ladies to converse, make music and play games, seated on the turf and chamomile benches. Adjoining it is the Knot Garden, a formal style in box, santolina, hyssop and wall germander, popular in Tudor and Stuart times.

35

TEA

The organic café overlooks the gardens and is open for morning coffee, lunches and tea. The freshly produced dishes and home-made cakes are created from the finest organic ingredients.

WEST COUNTRY AND SOUTHERN ENGLAND

The sites of the gardens shown on this map are approximate. They will give an indication as to how you might plan your visits. For precise instructions on finding the gardens, please refer to the specific information for each garden.

• Pengersick Castle

Old Mill Herbary •

ST AUSTELL.

• Eden Project

Rollmoon •

BARNSTABLE

BODMIN

EXETER

• Buckland Abbey

• Buckfast Abbey

Lytes Cary •

• Knightshayes

• Lower Severalls

• Gaulden Manor

MINEHEAD

DORCHESTER

POOLE

Dean's Court

Priest's House Museum & Gdn

Red House Museum & Gdn

• Cranborne Manor

• Braxton Gdns

• Tudor House Gdn

SOUTHAMPTON

PORTSMOUTH

Ventnor Botanic Garden

MALMESBURY

CIRENCESTER

• Cerney House Gdns

BRISTOL

BATH

• Abbey House Gdns

• Claverton Manor

Queen Eleanor's Gdn

READING

LONDON

• Gilbert White's Garden

• Petersfield Physic Gdn

The Herb Farm

• Losely Park

Abbey House Gardens

Market Cross, Malmesbury, Wilts SN16 9AS
Tel 01666 822212   www.abbeyhousegardens.co.uk

Follow the A429. From long stay car park in Malmesbury walk across Mill Lane Bridge and climb the 63 Abbey steps, or park in short-stay car park (2 hours max) from which it is a 2-minute walk

Open daily mid-Mar to mid-Oct 11–6; occasionally for NGS. Admission charge. Wheelchair access for most of garden
Owner Ian and Barbara Pollard

The garden once belonged to a Benedictine monastery and was, in part, the Abbot's garden, growing herbs, fruit trees, a vinery and roses. Ian Pollard has taken over the more or less derelict site and recreated the garden to reflect its history. Hedges break up larger areas and create separate rooms. There is much of interest. A yew hedge has been planted on the upper lawn to imitate the shape of the original Lady Chapel. A Dinosaur Grove contains trees that would have been alive at the same time as the dinosaurs as well as camellias, hydrangeas and acers. There are 2,000 different varieties of rose reflecting the delights of a Tudor pleasure garden. Plants are well labelled.

THE HERB GARDEN

The Herb Garden is a 100ft diameter garden located in what was once the monastery's orchard. It is contained by a circular colonnaded walk made from an oak-latticed polytunnel frame which supports apple cordons, pears, medlars and vines on an outer layer, including some old varieties that the monks would have used in medieval times, with roses and clematis climbing the internal perimeter. This garden took months to build and was initially a response to a 'planting time/thyme' clock. The Knot Garden is in the front (where visitors enter). It consists of a Celtic cross knot, the design of which was influenced by St Martin's Cross on Iona. This garden is planted with

38

cotton lavender, wall germander and box, all planted in 2000. A Saxon arch has a hedge planted to replace the wall that would once have been there. On the far side of the Herb Garden is a foliage garden with a laburnum walk and a mulberry tree.

TEA

Light refreshments from the tea room can be enjoyed anywhere in the garden or in the Belvedere Room with spectacular views of the river walk.

Braxton Gardens

(used to be Lyme Valley Herbs)
Lymore Lane, Milford-on-Sea, Hants SO41 OTX
Tel 01590 642008

Just off the A337 between Lymington and New Milton

Open daily in summer 10–5; in winter weather permitting, please phone first
Admission free, donations to NGS. Wheelchair access
Herb shop; bookshop; plant centre
Owner Alan, Angela and Bryn Edmonson

THE HERB GARDEN

Selection of unusual herbs, alpines and shrubs in a walled garden with a cooling pool. There are many roses including the Apothecary's rose and eglantine rose (whose leaves smell of apples) and over 100 David Austin English roses. An unusual knot garden was inspired by an old manuscript and planted with germander and cotton lavender. Altogether the rose garden holds almost 100 different roses and there are many late-flowering roses and other late flowering plants. Some unusual thistles, chocolate-scented *Cosmos atrosanguineus* and lemon verbena all grow here. Herbs are a speciality and there are many old-fashioned herbs tucked away in flower beds including angelica, fennel, comfrey, feverfew and mullein. There are eight varieties of thyme, all labelled, ranging from orange-scented to the creeping *Thymus serpyllum minimus* and many mints. The labelling is excellent.

TEA

Coffee and cream teas are served on the lawns or patios or in the shop if the weather is bad.

Buckfast Abbey

Buckfastleigh, Devon TQ11 0EE
Tel 01364 645 500   www.buckfast.org.uk

1/2 mile from the A38 dual carriageway, midway between Exeter and Plymouth

Open every day. Admission free. Wheelchair access
Gift shop; bookshop; monastic produce shop; restaurant
Owner Buckfast Community of Benedictine Monks

The Abbey, on the south eastern edge of Dartmoor was established as a Benedictine monastery in 1018. It joined the Cistercian Order in the twelfth century. At the dissolution of the monasteries in 1539, the monastery was closed down. In 1882 the site was bought by a group of monks who rebuilt it over 30 years. Today it is still home to a community of Benedictine monks. You can visit the beautiful Abbey Church, enjoy the exhibition about the Abbey's history, and buy various unique products made at the monastery including tonic wine, honey, biscuits, incense, candles, beauty products and pottery.

THE HERB GARDEN

From the car park there are open spaces to wander in with some splendid old trees all around the site. There are three gardens divided into distinct, small areas: a lavender garden, a sensory garden and a physic garden. The lavender garden in particular attracts the bees that make the famous Buckfast honey. There are many different varieties of lavender, some of which are difficult to grow. The sensory garden is an area for contemplation and peace. Following the pattern of the original Persian paradise gardens, it has a channel of water running down the centre. A chamomile seat surrounded by a trellis is covered in honeysuckle and roses. The physic garden has over 200 plants which would have been grown in a medieval monastic herb garden. It is divided into four sections, each containing its own category of herb: culinary, household, medicinal and poisonous plants. Among the medicinal plants are feverfew, agrimony, self-heal, chamomile and lavender. A generous arbour has fruit trees trained over it and the garden is rich in apple and pear trees and soft fruit bushes. There's an island of poisonous plants (in the middle of a pond so you can't test them).

TEA

The Abbey's Grange Restaurant offers traditional Devon cream teas, hot drinks and snacks throughout the day. You can also get lunch and light snacks. All food is prepared on the premises.

Buckland Abbey

Yelverton, Devon PL20 6EY
Tel 01822 853607   www.nationaltrust.org.uk

Signed from A386 at Yelverton

Open all year; dates and times vary so please check first.
Admission charge (NT members free); wheelchair access
Shop; plants for sale
Owner The National Trust

Buckland Abbey was originally a Cistercian abbey, founded 700 years ago. It became the home of Sir Francis Drake during the sixteenth century. There are extensive grounds and elaborate walks in which you can come across galvanized wire and other sculptures.

THE HERB GARDEN

The charming herb garden, planted by Vita Sackville-

West in the 1950s, runs along the side of the Great Barn and is redolent with scent and the hum of bees. It has over 54 different culinary and medicinal herbs. More recently, a thyme garden has been planted just round the corner. Equally interesting perhaps to herb lovers is the new Elizabethan garden. This is an unusual project for the National Trust in that rather than restoring the old garden they have created an entirely new layout to take the place of a line of 16 yew trees that succumbed to disease. Evidence from historical sources was the inspiration for this evolving garden, which aims to reflect the property's Tudor history. It has a circular pool, granite steps, topiary bushes, box-edged beds and plants from Tudor times. There is also a small orchard of old fruit cultivars.

TEA

National Trust quality home-made teas and light refreshments are available in the restaurant.

Cerney House Gardens

North Cerney, Cirencester, Glos GL7 7BX
Tel 01285 831300   www.cerneygardens.com

4 miles N of Cirencester past the church at North Cerney

Open Apr to Jul Tue, Wed, Fri 10–5 or by appointment
Admission charge. Wheelchair access to parts of garden
Plant sales, produce sales
Owner Sir Michael and Lady Angus

Secret gardens high above the Churn Valley. A 3¹/₂ acre red brick walled garden has many colourful borders and seating areas. There is a ha-ha, a duck pond, a gazebo walk, a knot garden and a laburnum arch. You can walk through the wildflower bank or go for a woodland walk. You may come across Oscar the peacock, also pigs and chickens. Lady Angus and her daughter Barbara have restored and enlarged the garden using organic methods, attracting butterflies and bees. The herbaceous borders have many old-fashioned favourites and are edged with lavender and hyssop. There are roses everywhere including rose-covered arches along the paths. The working kitchen garden and the orchard supply family, friends, visitors and some local businesses with produce.

THE HERB GARDEN

The well-labelled herb garden consists of two areas. One is medicinal, based on *Culpeper's Herbal*, it shows what the plants look like (no guarantees on reliability of any cures!). The other is culinary with a small area for teas, tisanes and the cloth industry.

TEA

The tea-room offers help-yourself tea and cakes when the garden is open. A more elaborate cream tea can be provided if you telephone first.

Claverton Manor

Claverton, Bath, Somerset BA2 7BD
Tel 01225 46050 www.americanmuseum.org

2 miles SE of Bath off the A36

Open grounds mid-Mar to end Oct Tue to Sun; closed Mon except bank holidays and Mon in August
Admission charge. Wheelchair access
Herb shop, plant sales
Owner The American Museum in Britain

Claverton Manor is a stone house built in the early part of the nineteenth century, now furnished to illustrate significant episodes in the development of American civilization including many beautiful patchwork quilts and a room of Shaker furniture.

THE HERB GARDEN

The house makes a stylish backdrop to the herb garden, which was a gift from the Southampton (New York) Garden Club. The garden is about 3.6m square and grows a surprisingly wide variety of useful plants in this modest space. The garden is paved with stone slabs edged with a double row of cobble stones. In the centre is a traditional beehive set among sweetly scented herbs within a circle of paving stones and bordered by wall germander and cotton lavender. Two stone paths lead to the centre and within the beds are to be found lemon thyme and lemon balm. Dye plants include woad, formerly used to achieve a rich blue colour, indigo and weld. Herbs from this garden are used to make the pretty posies or tussie mussies that are sold in the shop. The herbs in this garden are those that would have been carried over to America by the Pilgrim Fathers in the seventeenth century. More herbs are grown in the Mount Vernon garden, a gift from the Colonial Dames of America and a replica of George Washington's garden in Virginia with the same flowers he would have cultivated including roses and other colourful flowers growing in box-edged beds. The wide terrace running round the house is shaded by mop head bay trees.

TEA

A cup of tea with home-made cakes and scones can be savoured sitting on the terrace overlooking the spectacular view over the Avon Valley.

Cranborne Manor Gardens

Cranborne, Wimborne, Dorset BH21 5PP
www.cranborne.co.uk

18 miles N of Bournemouth

Open Wed only Mar to Sept 9–5. House not open.
Admission charge. Wheelchair access
Garden centre; gift shop
Owner The Marquess of Salisbury

The complex of individual gardens was laid out at the beginning of the seventeenth century as a formal garden with intricate parterres (now lawns). The gardens now include a walled vegetable garden, a yew bowling alley, croquet lawn, sundial garden (designed with a mount for surveying the countryside and laid out by John Tradescant during the reign of James I), white garden, orchard, pergola walk, and avenues.

THE HERB GARDEN

The green garden, chalk walk and herb garden are enclosed within tall yew hedges and provide a succession of treats discovered via narrow gateways in the yew. The Herb Garden was created in 1960. Its paths lead to a central stone sundial. The eight beds, arranged symmetrically, are edged with cotton lavender (*Santolina incana*). There is a large selection of culinary herbs as well as less usual herbs from the past including many sweetly scented plants surrounding the sundial. Six standard honeysuckles give height to the centre (an idea included in the herb garden at Hatfield House as well). Many varieties of thyme grow here as well as scented tulips and a long border of lily-of-the-valley edged with chives and backed by a rose hedge. The Walled Vegetable Garden was redesigned in 1999 with lavender and wildflower beds, vegetables for the house and flowers for cutting – all in a formal design. This is a relaxing garden in spite of its formality.

TEA

There is a pleasant tea room in the small, independent garden centre set in the old walled garden at Cranborne Manor, which specialises in old-fashioned roses and also sells clematis, herbaceous plants and shrubs. The gift shop is here as well. Open Mon to Sat during summer, Sun and bank holidays in winter. Tel 01725 517248 e-mail: gardencentre@cranborne.co.uk

Dean's Court

Wimborne, Dorset BH21 1EE
Tel 01202 882456

2 min walk from central Wimborne

Open Apr, May, Aug, Sep Sun 2–6; Mon 10–6 and
occasional days. Please telephone first
Admission charge. Wheelchair access
Organic plant and vegetable sales (usually)
Owner Sir Michael and Lady Hanham

The house was once the Deanery to the Minster. Now its 13 acres of partly wild gardens with fine specimen trees, lawns and borders constitute a welcome surprise – a peaceful haven near the centre of Wimborne.

THE HERB GARDEN

The old kitchen garden has a long serpentine (crinkle crankle) wall and some of the oldest varieties of vegetables grown as well as a superb collection of herbs. The gardens are chemical-free, and part of the Henry Doubleday seed bank of endangered botanical species is grown here. Chemical-free produce and herbaceous plants are usually available for sale.

TEA

Traditional cream teas are available on garden open days (lunch by negotiation).

Eden Project

Bodelva, St Austell PL24 2SG
Tel 01726 811911   www.edenproject.com

Follow the brown signs from the A30 and A390.

Open daily except 24–25 Dec summer 10–6, winter 10–4.30
Admission charge. Wheelchair access
Owner The Eden Trust

Famous for its biomes that look like enormous bubbles, the Eden Project is the brain child of Tim

Smit of Heligan fame. Its mission is 'to promote the understanding and responsible management of the vital relationship between plants, people and resources leading to a sustainable future for all'.

THE BIOMES

Eden is a very unconventional herb garden, nevertheless it focuses very much on 'useful' plants and is fascinatingly educational. The Humid Tropics Biome, the largest conservatory in the world, displays how rainforests contain thousands of different plant species of which, in some areas, fewer than 5 per cent have yet been tested for their medicinal properties. Conserving the rainforests' medicine chest may provide cures for today's illnesses. Here you will find orchids, cocoa, rubber, the Madagascar periwinkle (source of alkaloids used in treating leukaemia) ferns, buttress roots, and much, much more. The Warm Temperate Biome holds Mediterranean plants but also those from California, South Africa, South West Australia and Chile. The Outdoor Landscape holds plants from Britain, parts of America, Russia and the Indian foothills. A third biome is planned to represent the arid or desert zone. Permanent exhibits include Lavender, Dye Plants, Tea, Plants that Feed the World, Plants for Taste, Plants for Tomorrow's Industries and Hemp. The Asia Trail informs about indigo, peppers, sugar, garlic, cotton, coconut and rice – all grown in Asia – and at Eden.

TEA

A very acceptable cup of tea with cakes, biscuits and sandwiches and other light refreshments are available in the restaurant/café next to the interesting shop and with windows with a view over the biomes.

Gaulden Manor

Tolland, Lydeard St Lawrence, Somerset TA4 3PN
Tel 01984 667213

9 miles north west of Taunton off the A358 and B322

Open early Jun to end Aug, Sun, Thur and Bank Holiday
Mon; groups by appointment
Admission charge. Wheelchair access
Gardens; sometimes gardening books for sale
Owner Mr and Mrs James Starkie

Gaulden is a unique lived-in medieval manor, noted for early plasterwork. Here the Starkies have created a series of gardens from a paddock. These include a herb garden, a butterfly garden and a bog garden.

THE HERB GARDEN

The herb garden was planted in 1974. It is in the traditional shape of a cross or Paradise garden with four separate beds. There are ancient apple trees and an elder hedge, interspersed with hawthorn forming green and leafy boundaries. Brick paths separate the beds leading to a central sundial. The whole is surrounded by many shrub roses. A comfrey bed makes a tall splash of colour with a mixture of pink, white and purple flowers. The leaves, rich in potash, are used on the compost heap. The view garden, surrounded by shrub roses, is a restful place to sit and enjoy the surrounding hills.

TEA

Teas are not available within the garden but ten minutes away is Stable Cottage in the village of Triscombe, 1/2 mile to the NE of the Manor via the A358, which serves delicious cream teas in what used to be a stable block. It has a conservatory looking over generous gardens with wonderful views of the Quantocks and surrounding countryside. Open every day Apr to Oct and weekends in winter 2–5.30.
Tel 01984 618239.

Gilbert White's House

High Street, Selborne, Alton, Hants GU34 3JH
Tel 01420 511275

In centre of Selborne on B3006

Open Jan to Dec, daily 11–5.
Admission charge. Wheelchair access
Gift shop; plants for sale
Owner Oates Memorial Trust

This charming eighteenth-century house whose
rooms have been furnished in eighteenth-century
style, was the home of the Rev Gilbert White
(1720–1793) who meticulously recorded the natural
history of plants, animals and birds in his village.

THE HERB GARDEN

The garden is gradually being restored, displaying
plants and features described by White. Many of the
plants grown in the garden are, of course, herbs,
whether grown specifically in the herb garden or
elsewhere. There is a 'quincunx' orchard (trees laid
out in modules of the number 5), a wooden and
stone ha-ha and topiary. The 'Six Quarter' beds
display plants known to White in the eighteenth
century, all set among the original brick paths with a
sundial, a laburnum arch, a wild garden. The herb
garden itself is particularly fragrant.

TEA

The Tea Parlour in the restored dining room serves
home-made baking based on eighteenth-century
recipes.

The Herb Farm

Peppard Road, Sonning Common, Reading RG7 9NJ
Tel 0118 972 4220   www.herbfarm.co.uk

4 miles N of Reading on the B481 on the left

Open daily 10–5 (reduced hours Jan and Feb)
Admission free but small charge for the maze. Mainly

accessible to wheelchairs
Nursery; large shop with scented gifts, culinary delicacies,
skin care products.
Owner Richard Scott

The nursery was founded in 1985. It grows herbs,
stocks David Austen roses and has a comprehensive
range including many wild flowers, New English
roses and cottage garden plants. A knowledgeable
staff can offer helpful advice.

THE HERB GARDEN

Visitors can walk through the demonstration garden
which is filled with hundreds of aromatic, medicinal
and culinary herbs. There are also wildlife ponds and
a large symbolic Saxon hedge maze created in 1991
(summer only).

TEA

The Orangery coffee shop next to the gift shop in the
large barn, where you can get a variety of teas
including some herb teas, as well as home-made
scones and cakes. The gift shop offers an extensive
selection of herbal and garden products.

Knightshayes Walled Garden

Knightshayes Court, Bolham, Tiverton, Devon EX16 7RQ
Tel 01884 257381

2 miles N of Tiverton; turn right off Tiverton–Bampton road
(A396) at Bolham; 7 miles from M5 Junction 27 (A361)

Open Mar to Oct daily 11–5.30
Admission charge (NT members free). Partly accessible to
wheelchairs
Gift shop; guided tours by arrangement
Owner The National Trust

Knightshayes is a grand Victorian country house
designed by William Burgess for the Heathcoat-
Amory family. The celebrated garden features a
water lily pool, topiary, wonderful specimen trees,

rare shrubs, attractive woodland. Being on a slope it offers spectacular glimpses of the countryside.

THE HERB GARDEN

Since 2003 work has been undertaken to reinstate the enormous walled garden (fallow since 1964) as an organic vegetable and fruit garden. There are cooking and eating apples; old varieties of vegetables from various sources are used in the restaurant. A small vineyard will eventually supply grapes for local wine. Among this burgeoning plenty are two herb gardens. One consists of two wide borders running the whole sloping breadth of the garden with a path between. After just one year, the herbs were filling out the space, growing under dwarf apples and make a spectacular tapestry of varieties of lemon balm, angelica, poppies, chamomile, Jacob's ladder, mints, fennel, sweet cicely, chicory, goat's rue, cornflowers, alliums and dianthus, fuller's teasels and something called lady's maid (*Arum maculatum*).

The other herb garden, near the entrance, is for culinary herbs. It started as a 'holding area' because many people donated seeds and plants but now it is well-matured, gravelled and burgeoning with common and not-so-common herbs used for cooking. It is hoped there will eventually be enough to sell in Tiverton market. Volunteers are crucial to this garden and are always willing to talk to visitors.

TEA

You can take tea in Stables Restaurant, under cover or in the courtyard with home-made scones and a choice of cakes. Light lunches are also available. In October opening hours may vary. Please check.

Loseley Park Walled Garden

Guildford, Surrey GU3 1HS
Tel 01483 304440   www.loseley-park.com
Off B3000 at Compton, south of Guildford

Open May to Sep Wed to Sun 11–5, May and Aug Bank
Holiday Mon
Admission charge. Wheelchair access
Gift shop (also sells ice cream and other dairy and bakery
products); sale of plants raised in the gardens
Owner Michael More-Molyneux

Loseley is a dignified Elizabethan house set amid
splendid parkland. It was built in 1562 by a direct
ancestor of the present More-Molyneux family. The
sheltered Moat Walk is planted with long borders of
sun-loving plants.

THE HERB GARDEN

The 2^1/$_2$ acre Walled Garden (originally laid out in
1562) now contains five gardens based on a Gertrude
Jekyll design. The old yew hedges have been
drastically cut back and there's an old medlar tree
with a group of palms. The five gardens, each with its
own theme and character, are surrounded by a
magnificent old Vine Walk with a huge wisteria.
Redevelopment started in 1993/4 with the award-
winning Rose Garden, which has over 1,000
(meticulously labelled) old-fashioned rose bushes
contained within low clipped box hedges. Box balls
and circles create the framework and pillars of roses
and hollies add height. This was followed by the
Herb Garden, now well-matured, which is divided
into triangular beds in four separate sections
containing over 200 culinary, medicinal, household
and decorative herbs as well as others used in
cosmetics, lotions and dyes. The air is full of the
scent of rosemary, lavender and thyme. The gravel
paths are edged in terracotta shaded by acacia trees
where the main paths meet. There is also a Vegetable
and Cut Flower Garden. The tranquil Fountain
Garden has a white, silver and pale yellow theme.

TEA

The Courtyard Tea Room is in part of the old
kitchens and courtyard of the house itself and serves

a delicious selection of afternoon teas, also morning coffee and light lunches. (Chestnut Lodge Restaurant serves hot and cold lunches.)

Lower Severalls Nursery and Garden

Crewkerne, Somerset A18 7NX
Tel 01460 73234   www.lowerseveralls.co.uk

1 1/2 miles NE of Crewkerne on the road between Merriott and Haslebury Plucknett

Open mid Mar to end Sep Tue, Wed, Fri, Sat 10–5 (including bank holidays); May only Sun 2–5
Admission charge to garden. Wheelchair access Nursery
Owner Mr and Mrs Pring

THE HERB GARDEN

Enchanting and original 2 acre plantswoman's cottage garden developed over the last 25 years in front of an eighteenth-century Hamstone farmhouse. There is an informal atmosphere with profuse herbaceous borders, a green roofed pavilion, an enormous living dogwood basket, a wadi and a scented garden. Mary Pring, daughter of the owners, began growing herbs when she was quite young and they remain her true passion. She has now added herbaceous perennials and half-hardy plants and has an impressive catalogue of over 25 pages of plants. Culinary and scented herbs are a speciality of the garden, and the nursery specialises in herbs, herbaceous and conservatory plants. The herb list includes culinary, aromatic and medicinal plants and offers many interesting and unusual items. Lavender is a particular favourite and she has 21 varieties.

TEA

Bilby's Coffee Shop, Market Street, Crewkerne (Tel 01460 72622) on the main road in Crewkerne offers

speciality teas, cream teas, cakes and scones.
Strawberry Fayre, 12 Falkland Square, Crewkerne
offers cream teas with home-made cakes (Tel 01460
74539)

Lytes Cary Manor

Nr Charlton Mackrell, Somerton, Somerset TA11 7HU
Tel 01458 224471

*Signposted from Podimore Junction of A303, A37 take
A372*

Open Apr to Oct Wed, Fri, Sun 11–5 plus bank holiday Mon
Admission charge (NT members free). Gardens largely
accessible to wheelchairs.
Owner National Trust

Tudor home of the Lyte family for over 400 years. Sir
Henry Lyte cultivated a physic garden and published
his *Niewe Herball* in 1578 based on the plants he
grew here. Dedicated to Queen Elizabeth I from 'my
poore house in Lytescarie within your Majesties
Countie of Somerset the first day of Januarie
MDLXXVIII.'

THE HERB GARDEN

The garden consists of about 1.2 hectares in
compartments. Not much of the original garden
survives but under the National Trust Elizabethan
plants are grown such as catmint, rue, lilies,
southernwood, and sweet peas. One garden designed
by Graham Stuart Thomas has a wide border of
scented flowers and herbs, purple sage, *Rosa
rubrifolia* and white with silver plants. Well-trimmed
yew hedges with clipped buttresses form alcoves for
stone vases and provide shelter.

TEA

No refreshments are available at Lytes Cary itself but
The Buttercross Tea Rooms, Market Place,
Somerton are only a few minutes away and serve

good teas. Tel 01458 275168. Montacute House
(another NT property) is 6 miles away and serves
teas.

Old Mill Herbary

Helland Bridge, Bodmin, Cornwall PL30 4QR
Tel 01208 841 206   www.gardensincornwall.co.uk

*Access from A30 1 mile north of Bodmin and B3266
Bodmin to Camelford road*

Open Apr to Sep 10–5. Closed Wed.
Admission charge. Limited wheelchair access; no dogs
Plants for sale
Owner Mr and Mrs RD Whurr

THE HERB GARDEN

The garden has been created by the Whurrs since
1984. There are a number of sculptures centred
around a Greek/Roman Fertility theme and a rich
variety of plants to encourage the natural flora and
fauna. The garden stretches along a valley with about
three acres of semi-wild woodland walks
interspersed with islands and bridges along the River
Camel. There is a mini arboretum of about 1.25 acres
planted with over 40 unusual (labelled) trees in a
small level meadow adjoining the fifteenth-century
Helland Bridge. The Mill was demolished in the early
1930s but several large granite 'clapper' stones,
troughs and mushrooms still remain. The leat, fed by
a natural spring has been restored and feeds a
natural bog and water garden giving home to an
enormous variety of named planted displays of
culinary, medicinal and aromatic herbs, unusual and
rare species of wild flowers, shrubs, trees and
climbers. Throughout the garden are new and rare
species of herb, particularly those of medicinal
interest, which reflect the concern felt by the owners
for the conservation of the environment in which
they live. A walk along the terraced pathways leads to

the woodland area with wild daffodils, primroses, wood anemones, bluebells in spring and many varieties of fern. On one terrace is a chamomile lawn, releasing a delightful scent as one steps on it. The Whurrs have compiled a list of 50 medicinal plants grown in the garden with their Latin names and some of their medicinal properties.

TEA

If you ask nicely you may get a cup of tea served to you on the patio in return for a donation towards the garden. Otherwise there's a dearth of tea rooms unless you go into Bodmin (about 5 miles). Asda, Launceston Road, Nr Bodmin has a small coffee shop (Tel 01208 261800); or try Folly Tea Rooms, 3 Turf Street, Bodmin (Tel 01208 269250).

Pengersick Castle

Praa Sands, Breage, Cornwall TR20 9SJ
Tel 01736 762579

Off the A394 Helston–Penzance road

Open by appointment, please telephone for details
Admission fee; Wheelchair access
A resource centre has information about the site and the Tower may be visited.
Owner Mrs Angela Evans

Pengersick Castle and its tower were built in the sixteenth century as a demonstration of power. The place is a history lesson in its own right. The site has been inhabited since before the Middle Ages. Evidence suggests a Bronze/Stone Age settlement and shards of prehistoric pottery have been discovered. Pengersick is now run as an educational charity.

THE HERB GARDEN

A garden is being developed to portray the story of cultivation in England. This strip of land is unusually fertile for coastal Cornwall. A medieval garden was recreated several years ago on a site where such a garden might well have been, entered through a reconstructed archway. The design is based on the famous design for the Benedictine Monastery of St Gall (which was never actually built but remains a useful model). The planting is based on a plant list drawn up by Bishop Aelfric in 995 AD. A small Tudor knot garden has been planted modelled on Thomas Hill's A gardener's Labyrinth (1755). A well-established display of old roses links Pengersick to the Wars of the Roses.

TEA

Pengersick does not have a café but excellent teas are available about six miles away at Cripplesease Pottery Tea Room (Tel 01736 740004), Naclendra, Penzance TR20 8NF (about 3 miles from St Ives on the B3311); speciality teas, fruit teas, home-made scones, cakes and cream teas

Petersfield Physic Garden

16 The High Street, Petersfield, Hampshire
Tel 01730 269060

Behind the High Street in the centre of town

Open all year except Christmas Day and New Year's Day
10–6. Admission free. Wheelchair access
There are some good explanatory leaflets and a few herbs for sale
Owner Hampshire Gardens Trust

THE HERB GARDEN

Set in an ancient walled medieval plot, the garden has recently been planted in a style that would have been familiar to John Goodyer, the distinguished seventeenth-century botanist, who lived in Petersfield. The garden is just over a quarter of an acre and was given to Hampshire Gardens Trust in

1988 by Major John Bowen. Part of the garden is laid out with beds of herbs in a formal geometric pattern typical of seventeenth-century physic gardens. There are other features popular in gardens of this period such a small knot garden, a topiary walk, an orchard area underplanted with wild flowers, a rose bower with shrub roses, a sundial and terracotta urns. All the plants grown here would have been familiar to John Goodyer. The paths are suitable for wheelchairs and there are plenty of seats so that visitors can enjoy the garden and its plants.

TEA

The garden has no café but backs onto Petersfield High Street where there are plenty of places to choose from. The Folly Tearooms in the next alley, 5 Folly Lane (Tel 01730 267432) offers a variety of speciality teas, herbal teas, sandwiches and home-made cakes as well as breakfasts and lunches.

Priest's House Museum and Garden

The Museum of East Dorset Life, and Garden,
23–27 High Street, Wimborne Minster, Dorset BH21 1HR
Tel 01202 882533

In centre of Wimborne Minster

Open early Apr to end Oct Mon to Sat 10.30–5; also Jun to Sep Sun 2–5
Admission charge. Wheelchair access to garden
Shop; archaeological and childhood galleries; library; study facilities
Owner priest's House Museum Trust

This historic sixteenth-century town house is a Grade II* listed building housing an award-winning museum with period room settings.

THE HERB GARDEN

The 300m walled garden at the back of the house is a

WIMBORNE MINSTER • WINCHESTER

pleasant, well planted oasis in the heart of the
bustling town, with seats dotted around for quiet
contemplation. It is a long, narrow garden with
flowering plants growing among mature fruit trees,
topiary and lawns. There are a few unusual plants,
herbaceous and herb borders, all well cared for by
volunteers who are happy to answer questions about
the plants.

TEA

The 1920s Boathouse Tearoom, in the middle of this
charming garden, serves teas with home-made cakes
from Jun to Sep.

Queen Eleanor's Garden

The Great Hall, Winchester, Hants
Tel 01962 846476

Off the A3090 Romsey Road

Open daily 10–5. Closed Christmas Day and Boxing Day
and for occasional civic events
Shop
Owner Hampshire County Council

THE HERB GARDEN

Just outside the south door of Winchester's Great
Hall, tucked into a narrow space is Queen Eleanor's
garden. This is an accurate example of a medieval
pleasure garden and includes many features that
would have been present in the thirteenth century
and plants known to have been grown in that period.
A remarkable number of features can be found in
this small enchanted space. Thus you will find turf
seats, bay hedges, a fountain, a chamomile lawn,
tunnels, arbours and many herbs and flowers of the
time. It is a re-creation of a medieval herbarium
named after two queens, Queen Eleanor of Provence
wife of Henry III and her daughter-in-law Queen
Eleanor of Castile, wife of Edward I. The design was

inspired by surviving records of the royal garden including a herber or secluded sitting area. One interesting aspect is the garden's symbolic nature. Many plants were philosophically associated with religious or personal virtues. Among many symbolic plants are holly, ivy and bay (faithfulness).

TEA

No teas are available here but during the week the Guards Museum behind the Great Hall has a coffee shop and at weekends there are plenty of tea rooms and coffee shops in the town centre. The tranquil Cathedral Refectory in the Cathedral Visitor Centre (01962 857258) is tall and light with large windows and offers cream teas including Cathedral Blend and other varieties of tea.

Red House Museum and Garden

Quay Road, Christchurch, Dorset BH23 1BU
Tel 01202 482860

In the centre of Christchurch off A35

Open all year Tue to Sat 10–5 Sun 2–5; closed Good Fri. Admission charge. Wheelchair access to ground floor and garden
Gift shop; museum
Owner Hampshire County Museums Service

This modest red brick building was built as a workhouse in 1764. As a museum it covers archaeology, social history and costume with lots of archive material.

THE HERB GARDEN

This oasis of tranquillity in the heart of Christchurch has a central lawn with a rectangular pond and evergreen yews round the edges. Inside the walled garden is a collection of aromatic herbs and old-fashioned roses in raised beds, with a woodland walk in the South Garden.

TEA

There is a café in the museum courtyard where you can enjoy a cup of tea or coffee with sandwiches, cakes and scones.

Rosemoor Herb Gardens

RHS Garden Rosemoor, Great Torrington, North Devon
EX38 8PH
Tel 01805 624067

1 mile S of Great Torrington on the A3124 (formerly B3220); approx 1 hour from the M5 at Tiverton (Junction 27)

Open daily except Christmas Day; Apr to Sep, 10–6; Oct to Mar, 10–5; admission charge (RHS members free); wheelchair access throughout garden
Shop and plant centre
Owner Royal Horticultural Society

Rosemoor is rich in variety. The formal garden demonstrates a wide range of plants and planting styles in a series of garden rooms including the Queen Mother's Rose Garden for modern roses and its companion Shrub Rose Garden containing 130 cultivars. The winter interest is spectacular.

THE HERB GARDEN

The Cottage and Herb Gardens are more informal, separated by the Potager with its decorative vegetable planting. Here you will find a good variety of poisonous (often medicinal), culinary, dye and economic plants. There's an interesting collection of thymes, grown in pots because the heavy wet soil does not suit these Mediterranean herbs, as well as collections of mints and scented pelargoniums – also in pots so that people can touch and smell them easily.

TEA

Self-service licensed restaurant in the Robin Herbert Centre which has been extended and offers Devon cream teas and a wide range of delicious home-made lunches catering for vegetarians with specific dietary needs. Picnics are allowed in the picnic area near the car park.

Ventnor Botanic Garden

Undercliff Drive, Ventnor, Isle of Wight PO38 1UL
Tel 01983 855397
Open daily 10–6
Admission charge. Wheelchair access
Plant sales
Owner Isle of Wight Gardens Trust

The garden site was once the Royal National Hospital for Diseases of the Chest which was demolished in 1969. It has been redeveloped since 1989 and is now one of the youngest Botanic Gardens in Britain with a large collection of British native flowers.

THE HERB GARDEN

The medicinal garden is ornamental and includes historic herbal remedy plants formerly used in folk medicine, homeopathic medicine, medicinal plants used today and plants currently being investigated by drug companies. Medicinal plants come from all over the world including N American, Indian, Australian aboriginal, African, Maori, Chinese and European.

TEA

Tea and light refreshments are available in the modern new Visitor Centre.

CENTRAL ENGLAND

MANCHESTER

LIVERPOOL

CHESTER

Hardstoft
Herb Garden

LINCOLN

• Cheshire Blue
Lavender

Hardwick Hall

• Lincoln Cathedral
• Gunley Hall

NOTTINGHAM

Isaac
Walton Cottage •

Lavender Patch •

DERBY

Felley
Priory

WOLVERHAMPTON

LEICESTER

Astley Abbots •

BIRMINGHAM

• Prependal Manor House

BRIDGNORTH

• Castle Bromwich Hall Gdns

Birmingham Botanical
Gardens

• Ryton Herb Gardens

Mawley Hall

WORCESTER

• Coton Manor Gardens

• Shakespeare's Birthplace Gdns

Holdenby House •

NORTHAMPTON

CAMBRIDGE

GLOUCESTER

• Cowper &
Herb   Newton Museum
Society's • Toddington Manor
Nat. Herb • Stockwood Craft
Grdn   Museum & Gdns

• Selsley
Herb Nursery

OXFORD

National Herb Centre

Waltham
Place

BRISTOL

The sites of the gardens shown on
this map are approximate. They will give
an indication as to how you might plan
your visits. For precise instructions on
finding the gardens, please refer to the
specific information for each garden.

Alderley Grange

Alderley, Gloucestershire
Tel 01453 842161

Turn NW off A45 Bath to Stroud road at Dunkirk

Open by appointment only; also advertised in National
Garden Scheme yellow book
Owner Mr Guy and the Hon Mrs Acloque

THE HERB GARDEN

Enclosed by brick walls with many fine trees in the
middle of an English village this 4.5m square garden
is notable for its superb detail and meticulous
upkeep. The herb garden is a joy and there are also
lovely borders in other parts of the garden. Sweet
Williams, lady's mantle, evening primroses and
many shrub roses scent the whole garden. A small
orchard growing medlars, filberts and quinces was
planted in 1977 to celebrate the Queen's jubilee. The
herb garden is designed in a star shape with eight
segments. Narrow paths between clipped box edges
lead to a sundial at the centre. Numerous herbs
include alecost, bistort, borage, angelica, woodruff,
bergamot and purple sage. The pretty long-lasting
pink flowered rose 'Ispahan' has been planted near
the sundial and flowers throughout June.

TEA

No tea is available on the premises but Poppy's Tea
Shop, 58 Broad Street, Chipping Sodbury, about 5
miles away, offers speciality teas, cream teas and
light snacks in a light and airy room. Mon to Sat 8–5
(Tel 01454 313328).

Astley Abbots Lavender Farm

Bridgenorth, Shropshire WV16 4SW
Tel 01746 763122   www.angelfire.com/blues/astleyabbotts
Just N of Bridgenorth off B4373

Open lavender fields Jul and Aug 10–5; also farm open by appointment throughout the year for sale of products. Admission to lavender farm free; admission charge to garden.

Small shop with lavender products; plants for sale; PYO

Owner Natalie Hodgson

THE HERB GARDEN

Natalie Hodgson started the lavender farm with only a few plants. She has since expanded the farm to over 4 acres of lavender with a five-acre garden nearby. She grows several species of lavender including white and pink varieties. The garden contains magnificent trees in picturesque surroundings and an interesting herb section with at least 100 varieties of herbs. In the lavender field is a solar powered drying shed. There is also a bee village where bees live in unusual homes and there are often observation hives where visitors can watch the bees at work. You can pick your own lavender in July and August.

TEA

Tea, coffee, chocolate and fruit drinks with home-made biscuits and cakes are available in the specially designed tea room and shop in which the hot water is heated by photovoltaic cells

Birmingham Botanical Gardens & Glass Houses

Westbourne Road, Edgbaston, Birmingham B15 3TR
Tel 01214 541860 www.birminghambotanicgardens.org.uk

Follow brown tourist signs in Edgbaston

Open all year except Christmas Day 9 (10 on Sat) –7 or dusk if earlier

Admission charge. Wheelchair access

Gift shop, plants for sale

Owner Birmingham Botanical & Horticultural Society

THE HERB GARDEN

These gardens were originally laid out as a public park by leading garden planner, journalist and publisher John Claudius Loudon in 1832. Their main objective is the study of plants discovered in the 'New Worlds' in the sixteenth century. There are many fine trees and shrubs, a pinetum and the main lawn is laid out as an amphitheatre. This historic layout remains much the same except for the four stately glasshouses (tropical, subtropical, Mediterranean and arid) which were added about 50 years later. The Mediterranean House grows citrus fruits of all sorts, pomegranates, olives, figs and liquorice. Economic plants to be seen include rice, papyrus, coffee, sugar, bananas and pineapples. There is a collection of 17,000 species of orchids. The Herb Garden has a wide variety of culinary, medicinal and ornamental herbs. Three historic gardens include a Roman, a Mediterranean and a Tudor Garden, all of which feature contemporary herbs. A Children's garden for 3–6 year olds show how plants work. Designed in the shape of a flower, each petal contains interactive exhibits. Ancient and modern roses abound.

TEA

The Pavilion Restaurant offers fresh coffee, teas and light lunches; many visitors enjoy picnics on the lawn.

Castle Bromwich Hall Gardens

Chester Road, Castle Bromwich, West Midlands B36 9BT
Tel 01217 494100   www.cbhgt.colebridge.net

5 miles from city centre just off B4114

Open Apr to Sep Wed to Fri 12–4; Bank Holiday Mon 1–5
Admission charge. Wheelchair access
Gift shop; plant sales; guided tours
Owner Castle Bromwich Hall Gardens Trust

THE HERB GARDEN

The house, built in 1599 and later extended is not open to the public. But here are 10 acres of listed Grade II* English baroque gardens developed by several generations of the Bridgeman family (later Earls of Bradford). The gardens were originally created by some of the outstanding artists, craftsmen and designers of their time and are in the process of being restored as closely as possible to the period of their heyday, 1680 to 1740, by a privately funded trust. In the 1980s archaeologists began to uncover this garden of national importance under a carpet of weeds and moss. Herbs abound in this garden. There are over 600 species of plants from the period. There is also a holly walk, a nineteenth-century holly maze designed by the famous London nurserymen George London and Henry Wise (laid out in a distorted image of the famous maze at Hampton Court). Fruits within the orchards and along the paths include apple, pear, apricot, quince, medlar, fig and cherry. Many historic vegetables and herbs are grown in the vegetable garden including the black 'Congo' potato and white carrots. The South Kitchen Garden has been created to a 1728 design by Batty Langley. The restoration is ongoing. The North garden will be laid out to a design shown in Henry Beighton's *South Prospect* of 1726 and has a parterre outlined with yew.

TEA

There is a courtyard coffee shop offering teas and light refreshments.

Coton Manor Gardens

Coton, Nr Guilsborough, Northants NN6 8RQ
Tel 01604 740219 wwwcotonmanor.co.uk
Between Northampton and Rugby; 5 miles from M1

*(Junctions 16 or 18); 4 miles from A14; signed from A5199
and A428*

Open Apr to Sep Tue to Sat and bank holiday weekends;
also Sun in Apr and May 12–5.30
Admission charge. Wheelchair access to principal areas
Gift shop; gift vouchers; plants for sale
Owner Ian and Susie Pasley-Tyler

THE HERB GARDEN

Coton Manor is a seventeenth-century manor house
in mellow stone with a 10 acre garden landscaped at
different levels on a hillside. The garden was laid out
in the 1920s and 30s by the grandparents of the
present owner and continues to be developed. A
number of smaller areas within the site gradually
unfold. There is a 5 acre bluebell wood (best in early
May), an apple orchard with 80 or so old English
varieties and a wildflower meadow. Coton is noted
for its luxurious borders, unusual plants and colour
and interest at all seasons. The Water Garden
consists of pools and streams wending their way
downhill from the pond and has primulas,
hellebores, ferns, hostas and geums. The Lawn
Border is very large and best in July and August with
deep pink and purple roses and many other species
and unusual plants. The Woodland Garden is host to
more shade-loving plants such as hellebores,
anemones and many more. The Holly Hedge Border
is a long, narrow border with herbaceous plants that
look their best in June and July such as dictamnus,
delphiniums, campanulas, salvias and much more.
The Herb Garden itself was designed by head
gardener Richard Green and planted in 1994. It
consists of ten beds edged with box and germander
with a wide range of culinary and medicinal herbs.
There are new yew hedges on two sides and
espaliered apple trees next to the entrance flanked by
the Rose Walk. In the Rose Garden the rose beds
form a circle quartered by brick paths where pink
'Mary Rose' and white 'Winchester Cathedral'

harmonise with pink and white peonies, along with geraniums, alchemillas, dianthus, violas and artemisias. There are many other roses and lots of clematis. The Medieval Bank with a sheltered, south facing aspect is a haven for grey-leafed plants such as lavenders, artemisia, santolina, cistus, melianthus, acanthus and eryngium. It was designed in expectation of warmer, drier summers arising from climate change. Over a thousand different plant varieties are available in the nursery, mostly grown in the garden.

TEA

The Stables Tea Room offers teas including Earl Grey, home-made scones, freshly made sandwiches and home-made light luncheon dishes. You can sit outdoors under a large black walnut tree or in the converted stables themselves.

Cowper and Newton Museum

Orchard Side, Market Place, Olney, Bucks MK46 4AJ
Tel 01234 711516   www.mkheritage.co.uk/cnm

Olney is on the A509 5 miles N of Newport Pagnell and Junction 14 of the M1

Open Mar to Dec Tue to Sat 10–1 and 2–5; Jun, Jul, Aug as before plus Sun 2–5, Bank Holiday Mon and Shrove Tue (Pancake Day). Admission charge; Wheelchair access to garden only
Museum shop; plant sales
Owner Cowper and Newton Museum Trust

THE HERB GARDEN

Orchard Side was the home of the eighteenth-century poet, letter-writer and classical scholar (and author of *John Gilpin*) William Cowper. The Cowper and Newton Museum is an independent museum run as a charitable trust with many interesting artefacts relevant to his life and the life of his friend and neighbour the Rev John Newton. (Cowper and

Newton paid a guinea a year (£1.05) for the right to cross an orchard between their two gardens when they visited one another.) This restored seventeenth-century garden is very much a garden full of herbs. You will find mainly plants known in Britain before the poet's death in 1800, including native plants, herbs brought back by the Romans and Crusaders from the Holy Land, and plants brought back from the New World before and during Cowper's lifetime. Careful research ensures that only the earliest varieties of those pre-1800 introductions are used. Cowper's love of wildlife and nature is reflected in the pond area of the garden, and the planting along the West Wall attracts birds, butterflies and other creatures. The restoration work was begun in 1994 with professional help from Sue Fisher and Ken Hollinshead. The ongoing work by volunteer gardeners is financed through plant sales. The existing concrete paths were retained for access to the whole garden and suitability for wheelchairs. All the plants are clearly labelled in yellow with black lettering with the date of introduction to this country.

The second garden at Orchard Side is more of a vegetable garden with a charming small summerhouse which Cowper called his 'verse manufactory'. Over the fence is Guinea Orchard and beyond it, the Old Vicarage, former home of his friend Newton.

TEA

There is no tea shop at the Museum itself but Teapots (Tel 01234 712392) is a courtyard restaurant close by in the Market Square of this pretty Georgian town and serves tea including herbal and fruit, and home-made cakes and scones.

Felley Priory Garden

Underwood, Nottinghamshire NG16 5FL
Tel 01773 810230

*About 3 minutes from Junction 27 of the M1 on the A608
going west*

Open all year Tue, Wed, Fri 9–12.30; Mar to Oct every
second and fourth Wed 9-4; every third Sun 11–4 and
occasionally at other times (please ring for details)
Admission charge. Wheelchair access
Plant sales
Owner Hon Mrs Chaworth Musters

Felley Priory was founded in 1156 and dissolved by
Henry VIII in 1536. At the time a new smaller house
was built which was added to in the nineteenth
century.

THE HERB GARDEN

Work on the present garden began in 1976. A
framework of hedges was planted for shelter, then
the herbaceous borders and after that the rest of the
garden has taken shape. All the compartments are
divided by evergreen hedges, but clipped in such a
way that they are not just divisions but allow
glimpses through to other parts of the garden and to
the wider, very beautiful countryside. There is also
an orchard and a young arboretum with some
uncommon trees including some unusual sweet
chestnuts and a ginkgo. Although not a herb garden
as such, there are well over 60 herb genera
represented in this stylish and enchanting garden
and anyone with an interest in herbs as decorative
plants will find it fascinating. There are many
herbaceous borders full of colour and unusual and
interesting plants including many salvias, and
varieties of origanum. There are pergolas, mainly
covered with roses, vines, clematis and honeysuckle
and knot gardens of architectural box. The gardens
round the walls have a mixture of small trees and
shrubs, underplanted mostly by hellebores, hostas,

digitalis, meconopsis and geraniums. The rose garden has about 90 different old-fashioned roses: Gallicas, Bourbons, Damasks, Albas, Chinensis and moss roses, many of them from nurseries in France. The medieval garden has flowers known in the fifteenth century including roses, lilies, violas, columbines, irises and tulips. All the plants in the nursery, mostly old-fashioned and unusual, are grown in the garden. In the plan of the garden given to visitors all the borders are numbered and in the nursery there is a list of the plants in the numbered borders as an aid to buying.

TEA

Delicious home-made teas including cream teas, served in pretty china are available in high season and also soup and light lunches.

Gunby Hall Herb Garden

Gunby Hall, Gunby, Nr Spilsby, Lincs PE23 5SS
Tel 01909 486411

2$\frac{1}{2}$ miles NW of Burgh-le-Marsh, 7 miles W of Skegness on S side of the A158

Open Apr to late Sep Wed and Thur 2–6. Admission charge (NT members free). Wheelchair access
Owner National Trust

THE HERB GARDEN

Gunby Hall is a plum-coloured Georgian brick mansion set in English parkland. There is a lot of lawn and a famous orchard. The herb garden is a more recent and very attractive feature. It forms a square of about 13.7m square. Stone slabs make the pathways with borders of chives and marjoram. A tapering border holds many vigorous herbs such as elecampane, balm, mint and lady's mantle. This runs along one of the ancient walls and is divided from the main herb area by a grass path. In one plot wormwood, monkshood, catmint, marjoram, globe artichoke, balm and golden and common sage grow vigorously. In another southernwood, parsley, tree onion, camphor, lovage, soapwort, sweet cicely, cotton lavender, tansy, bronze fennel, hyssop and sage provide a pattern of greys and greens. Rosemary, lavender, curry plant, wild marjoram, tarragon, lungwort, thyme, alkanet, iris and many types of mint are planted in profusion. Corner beds contain lavender, honeysuckles and ancient roses, old-fashioned fruit trees arched and in pyramids, central beds of catmint grow round a sundial.

TEA

Surprisingly, for an NT property, there are no refreshments at Gunby Hall. Chuzzlewit's Tea Room, 27 Upgate, Louth, about 10 miles away, may be your best bet. This is a family run traditional tea room offering quality teas and coffees including Japanese Cherry and China Rose Petal in china pots. Also freshly baked cakes, cream teas and sandwiches. Open Tues to Fri 10–4.30; Sat 9–5.30. Tel 01507 611171.

Hardstoft Herb Garden

Hall View Cottage, Hardstoft, Pilsley, Derbyshire S45 8AH
Tel 01246 854268

On the B6039 Holmewood to Tibshelf road, approx 2 miles from Junction 29 of the M1

Open 15 Mar to 15 Sep daily 10–5; closed Tue
Small admission charge. Wheelchair access (though gravel in car park can be awkward)
Herb-related gift shop; nursery
Owner Lynne and Steve Raynor

THE HERB GARDEN

First opened in 1983, Hardstoft is now one of the foremost herb nurseries in the country. The Raynors have divided the 1/2 acre plot of heavy clay soil with

Leyland cypress and thuja hedging to create gentler micro-climates and paving to absorb the sun's warmth. Over 200 varieties of herbs seen in the garden are available in the nursery. There are also spectacular areas of native flowers and wild spring bulbs from March to September. The labelling in Latin and English is excellent and you will find information posters giving details of the history and present day uses of herbs in medicine, cooking and perfumery.

The garden consists of four display gardens, the largest being the Mixed Herb Garden which now has a mature parterre. Here you will find dye plants such as woad (*Isatis tinctoria*) and madder (*Rubia tinctorum*). Each category is given four beds around a central bird bath. Height is added by *Rosa* 'Ballerina' trained as a standard. Herbaceous borders flank the sides of this garden. The Physic Garden, south of the parterre contains many rare and unusual medicinal plants from all over the world including some poisonous varieties. It is protected by a hedge of x *Cupressocyparis leylandii* with the medicinal beds radiating from a sundial. Brick paths divide beds of marigolds, meadowsweet, valerian and wormwood, evening primrose and other less common medicinal herbs. Hardstoft holds the National Collection of Echinacea including *E. tennesseensis* which is almost extinct in the wild. The Lavender Garden has one of the most comprehensive collections of the lavender family in the country with over 40 different varieties (here the fragrance is at its most overwhelming in July and August). The Pot Pourri Garden specialises in plants which dry well for pot pourri and flower arranging. Among the plantings are very rare and unusual species.

TEA

The Tea Room at Hardstoft (closed Mondays and Tuesdays except bank holidays) offers home-made recipes, many containing fresh home grown herbs from the gardens. A range of home-baked cakes is a speciality and includes lavender cake, rosemary fruit slice and cheese and herb scones.

Hardwick Hall Herb Garden

Doe Lea, Chesterfield, Derbyshire S44 5QJ
Tel 01246 850430

Junction 29 of M1; 6 miles NW of Mansfield by A617 and minor roads

Open garden 31 Mar to 31 Oct Wed, Thur, Sat, Sun 12–5.30
Shop, licensed restaurant
Owner National Trust

THE HERB GARDEN

Bess of Hardwick's sixteenth-century house flaunted her initials in the roof and was known in its time as the house of glass because of its many windows. The 2.8 hectares of gardens are small, enclosed in Tudor stone courts. One of them is a herb garden. The herb garden has been reconstructed in Elizabethan style. It is divided into two identical sections, each linked by a square central bed surrounded by a wide gravel path. The wide borders around these two square beds contain a rich mix of culinary herbs of the varieties most likely to have been used in a Tudor kitchen. Many half-hardy plants thrive; even pineapple sage, lemon verbena (*Lippia citriodora* syn. *Aloysia triphylla*), bay and myrtle do well. Italian lavender (*Santolina neapolitana*) flourishes here too.

TEA

Afternoon teas are available in the restaurant in the original kitchen with home-made scones and cakes and a choice of tea and herbal teas.

Herb Society's National Herb Garden

Sulgrave Manor, Sulgrave, Nr Banbury OX17 2SD
Tel 01295 768899   www.herbsociety.org

Just off the B4525 between Banbury and Northampton;
Junction 11 of M40; 10 miles west of Towcester and the A5

Open 1 Apr to 31 Oct 2–5.30
Admission charge (Herb Society members free). Limited
wheelchair access
Sulgrave shop; Herb Society shop
Owner herb garden leased to the Herb Society by the
Sulgrave Trust

THE HERB GARDEN

In 2002 the Herb Society was offered space for new
headquarters at Sulgrave Manor, the home of George
Washington's ancestors, owned and run by the
Sulgrave Trust. The Tudor house at Sulgrave is well
worth a visit, and its gardens are charming with an
orchard and a formal Italianate garden laid out in the
1920s by Sir Reginald Blomfield. This includes a
level garden with herbaceous beds, clipped yew
hedges and a clipped box parterre. The Sulgrave
Trust offered the Herb Society an L shaped plot of
land to create its own herb garden. The first part of
this garden, opened to the public in 2003, has an
arbour at each end. The planting has been designed
to reflect the ties between America and Britain and
the Tudor history of the garden. The central circular
bed is symbolic of the globe which the early pioneers
sailed round to find a new world. Here are the
medicinal and household herbs that would have been
carried over to America by these early settlers, for
example borage, self-heal, pot marigolds, woodruff,
thyme, savory and hyssop. Herbs that came from the
Americas are planted in separate beds and include
nasturtiums, sunflowers and other plants mentioned
in John Josslyn's *New England's Rarities
Discovered*, written fifty years after the 1620

landings in America and many other sources of
reference. The herbs are mostly 'official' herbs, that
is species or older forms denoted as *officinalis* in the
pharmacopoeias.

TEA

A very good tea, including various herbal choices is
available in the restaurant with delicious home-made
scones and cakes.

Holdenby House Gardens

Holdenby, Northants NN6 8DJ
Tel 01604 770074   www.holdenby.com

6 miles NW of Northampton off A5199 or A428

Open Jul and Aug Sun to Fri 1–5; Apr to Sep also Sun and
Bank Holiday Mon
Admission charge. Wheelchair access
Souvenir and craft shop (some exclusive to Holdenby);
falconry centre; rare breeds
Owner Mr and Mrs James Lowther

THE HERB GARDEN

Holdenby House was built in the sixteenth century
by Sir Christopher Hatton to entertain Elizabeth I. It
became the palace of James I and the prison of
Charles I. It is now a Victorian family house and
garden with Elizabethan remains. There are 20 acres
of stately lawns, hedges and gardens, the framework
of an Elizabethan bowling alley, and parterres and
terraces enclosing delightful modern planting.
An Elizabethan Garden was replanted in 1980 by
Rosemary Verey using plants which would have been
available in 1580, arranged round a central sundial
with clipped box and bay. The Fragrant Border was
planted by Rupert Golby and the now well
established **Silver Border**, not far from the
Falconry Centre, is home to a growing collection of
silver-leafed, white-flowered plants grown against a
tall stone wall. A Walled Garden provides fruit and

vegetables for the owners and is home to a collection of medicinal plants. Finely clipped yew hedges frame different sections of the garden. James and Karen Lowther work closely with garden designers to reflect Holdenby's historical associations as well as their own garden philosophies and ideas.

TEA

The Victorian Tea Room is open for cream teas when the gardens are open and there are places to picnic. (Meals for pre-booked groups available by prior arrangement.)

Izaak Walton Cottage Herb Garden

Izaak Walton Cottage, Shallowford, Nr Stone, Stafford
ST15 OPA   Tel 01785 619130

S of the A520 Stone to Eccleshall road

Open May to Aug weekends only 1–5
Admission free. Limited wheelchair access; gravel car park
Gift shop; books to browse
Owner Staffordshire Borough Council

THE HERB GARDEN

An enchanting small cottage typical of the sort of house that would have been on the estate of the local seventeenth-century author of *The Compleat Angler*. The garden concentrates on plants known in this country before the eighteenth century. There is a lawn and beds filled with early native roses and herbs surrounded by a yew hedge. Plants include borage, creeping Jenny, thyme, valerian, tansy, sorrel, St John's wort, feverfew, periwinkle, germander, rue, vervain and meadowsweet. Poppies, polyanthus, roses, bergamot, valerian and evening primroses add lots of colour. The garden is maintained by Meadowvale Herbs, who provide the plants.

TEA

Teas are available in a small refreshment room on site. (Gardening and herbal books are displayed here for visitors to browse through.) Or you can try the Grove Coffee House, St Mary's Grove, Stafford, about 7 miles away. Tel 01785 252825.

Lavender Patch

At Hall Croft Farm, Uttoxeter Road, Hilton, Derby DE65 5FZ
Tel 07815 956626   email:info@thelavenderpatch.com;
www.thelavenderpatch.com

Just outside Derby, Junction 24 on M1, follow signs for A50 Stoke on Trent/Uttoxeter then take exit for Hilton past Talbot and Kings Head pubs

Open Jul and Aug Wed to sun 12–5
Good wheelchair access with broad, flat path
Shop with fresh or dried herbs and lavender products including honey
Owner Sally Hibbert

THE HERB GARDEN

The Lavender Patch first opened in 2005. It was inspired by a visit to a lavender garden in the North of England and has been lovingly created from a wilderness of nettles, weeds and rabbits. There is a small field dedicated to lavender, full of butterflies, and bees. There is a raised sensory border in the middle of the garden. There are two varieties of French lavender grown to encourage wildlife and demonstrate how it can enhance a garden but also for texture 'and sheer decadence'. These are 'Fathead': 12in tall with dark purple flowers with purple topknots; 'Avonview', slightly taller with a strong scent, good for hedging. Other varieties are 'Imperial Gem' – the most popular: 18in tall with dark purple blooms and intense fragrance; 'Hidcote': 20in tall, superb dark blue blossoms, dries well; 'Grosso': 21in, with dark purple blooms, good for oil and pot pourri; 'Hidcote Pink': similar to Hidcote but candy floss pink; 'Miss Katherine': another sumptuous pink, good in salads and 'Grosso Alba', a tall, slender icicle-like plant.

TEA

Home-made teas are served next to the Garden Room (which is also the shop) and are thus accompanied by the smell of lavender.

Lincoln Cathedral

Lincoln LN2 1PZ
Tel 01522 544544   www.lincolncathedral.com

In the centre of the city

Open every day 7.15–8 (summer); 7.15–6 (winter)
Admission charge. Wheelchairs enter through West Front Cathedral shop
Owners The Dean and Chapter

THE HERB GARDEN

The Mary Garden at Lincoln Cathedral was planted by John Codrington of the Lincoln Herb Society in the mid 1900s in the cloisters of the Cathedral. The Cathedral is dedicated to St Mary and the garden created among its impressive pillars has plants partly chosen for their sweet scents and partly for their associations, through tradition and legend,z with the Virgin Mary, many of these are centuries old and found not only in England but throughout Christendom. After the Reformation the expression 'Our Lady' was frowned on in England as were too frequent references and allusions to the Blessed Virgin Mary. So some of these plants became simply lady's smock, maiden pink, and so on. Some even reverted to the pagan goddess Venus as in Venus's comb, a little cornfield weed akin to cow parsley or Venus's looking glass, an annual related to campanula. Only a few are listed here. They include our lady's ribbon or gardener's garters *Phalaris arundinacea picta*; our lady's thimble (harebell) *Campanula rotundifolia*; our lady's bedstraw *Galium verum*; our lady's lace (woodruff) *Asperula odorata*; our lady's keys (cowslip), *Primula vera*; our lady's glove, (foxglove) *Digitalis* and so on. There are also our lady's bells (snowdrop); lungwort (blue flowers for Mary and red for Joseph), our lady's tears (lily of the valley); marigold *Calendula officinalis* which represents Mary's gold or the golden rays of glory round her head.

TEA

Teas, hot meals and snacks are available in the Refectory near the Cathedral shop. Pimento Tearooms, 26/27 Steep Hill, Lincoln just down the hill from the Cathedral offers an excellent selection of teas and coffees. The upper rooms serve cakes and drinks, the lower room light vegetarian snacks. There is a garden and newspapers to read. Open Mon to Sat 10–5, Sun 10.30–5. Tel 01522 569333.

Mawley Hall Herb Garden

Mawley Hall, Cleobury Mortimer, Worcestershire DY14 8PN
Tel 01299 270869   www.mawley.com

1 mile N of Cleobury Mortimer on the A4117 and 7 miles W of Bewdley

Open on selected days during the summer and by appointment.
Owner Trustees of the Galliers-Pratt family

THE HERB GARDEN

Mawley Hall was built in 1730 and contains one of the finest Baroque interiors in England. By the late 1950s it was derelict. It was acquired by the Trustees of the Galliers-Pratt family who restored it under the direction of Anthony Galliers-Pratt. Rupert Galliers-Pratt now lives at Mawley with his family. The gardens were laid out in the 1960s and incorporate large expanses of lawn, parterres, vistas, urns, monuments, a tree for every letter of the alphabet and a herb garden. In 1969 this garden was created on a site previously occupied by old yew trees. Five pillars of Irish juniper line each side of the central path leading to the Joiner's Shop. The many long narrow beds are divided by equally narrow gravel paths. The herb garden is a tranquil and pleasantly scented area in which to relax but it is also very much a culinary herb garden and nearly all the herbs are used in the Mawley kitchens. There are over thirty herbs including chamomile and rosemary which are dried for herb pillows. Elecampane root is used for healing purposes, black peppermint to flavour ice-cream, lovage flavours chicken dishes and chervil is added to salads.

TEA

Mamble Craft Centre Tea Room, Church Lane, Mamble, Bewdley, less than 5 miles away off the A456, is in a seventeenth-century barn with oak beams and views to the Welsh mountains. It offers traditional Earl Grey and Darjeeling teas, herb teas, cream teas and a delicious choice of cakes. Open Tues to Sun 10.30–5. Tel 01299 832834.

The National Herb Centre

Banbury road, Warmington, Warks OX17 1DF
Tel 01295 690999   www.herbcentre.co.uk

Just outside Warmington village on the B4100, approximately 5 miles N of Banbury and 11 miles S of Warwick

Open daily, Mon to Sat, 9–5.30, Sun and bank holidays 10.30–5.30
Admission free. Wheelchair access
Plant Centre; Gift shop; Deli shop
Owner Nick Turner

THE HERB GARDEN

A herb plant centre and gift shop, herb display gardens, children's area, and nature trail. There are five display gardens designed by Simon Hopkinson, demonstrating herbs used in various everyday settings including the back garden of a new house, reclaimed drained land, and a paved garden with creeping thymes growing through the cracks in the paving.

TEA

Cream teas and home-made cakes are available in the attractive licensed Herb Bistro, located in a converted barn. It also serves a lunchtime menu including hot meals and puddings, home-made soup with herb bread and scones, savouries and snacks, and fresh baguettes to eat in or take out. The children's menu includes a Little Munchers Box, available all day (Tel 01295 690033).

Oxford Botanic Garden

The University of Oxford Botanic Garden, Rose Lane, Oxford OX1 4AZ

Tel 01865 286 690   www.botanic-garden.ox.ac.uk

In the centre of Oxford near Magdalen Bridge

Open Apr to Nov daily 9–5; Dec to Mar Mon to Fri 10–4.30
Admission charge. Wheelchair access.
Owner University of Oxford

THE HERB GARDEN

This $4^1/_2$ acre patch of land lying next to the river Isis is the oldest botanic garden in Britain, founded in 1621 to grow plants for practical, scientific and research purposes. Today plants are grown to support the university's teaching programmes and for scientific research but the plants are arranged attractively. Gardeners visit the garden for inspiration and visitors may easily find plants that would grow well in their own gardens at home. It consists of three sections: the glasshouse; the area outside the walled garden with a water garden and rock garden, an innovative black border and autumn border; and the walled garden itself. Here you can see the most diverse yet compact collection of plants in the world. The original wall surrounding this part of the garden is built in local Headington stone. Much of the area is taken up by long narrow family borders, the core collection of hardy plants. Other plants are arranged according to country of origin, botanic family or economic use. The Economic Quarters hold plants such as weld and woad used for dyeing and plants for making fibres. The Geographical Borders are planted according to where the plants originated. One bed is devoted to culinary herbs. The walled garden also houses the oldest tree in the garden, an English yew (*Taxus baccata*).

TEA

No tea is available at the Botanic Garden but there are plenty of places to have tea in the High Street. If you are going North try the Park House Tea Room and Antiques, 26 Park Street, Bladon (opposite St Martin's church on the A4095) which offers a good variety of teas. Open Mon to Fri 10–5.30; Sat and Sun 10–6. Tel 01993 813888.

Prebendal Manor House

Church Street, Nassington, Northants PE8 6QG
Tel 01780 782575   www.prebendal-manor.co.uk

A few miles from the A1 and A605 and well signposted from nearby villages

Open Easter Bank Holiday Mon to end Sep every Wed and Sun and Bank Holiday Mon 1–5.30
Admission charge (includes audio tour). Wheelchair access
Museum
Owner Jane Baile

THE HERB GARDEN

The Prebendal Manor House is the earliest surviving dwelling in Northamptonshire, part of a collection of ancient stone buildings. Enjoy a leisurely walk through this most attractive and fascinating reconstruction of a medieval garden, planted in 1985. Visitors are given a copy of the plan and information about the plants seen on the walk which includes ancient fish ponds, orchards and culinary and medicinal herbs. The plants have been selected from several plant lists which include the earliest English gardening book by 'Jon Gardener' and a fifteenth-century 'Leech book' containing medicinal recipes used by Nicholas Colnet, physician to Henry V in 1415. Nicholas was given the Prebendal Manor in 1417, presumably for services rendered. The garden is best from late May to mid-Jul as the medieval flowers largely used are not repeat-flowering. The garden's designer, Mike Brown has added a wild garden on the site to provide longer-lasting flowering period.

TEA

Speciality teas including herb teas are available with very delicious home-made cakes served within the large tithe barn where there is also a museum showing the archaeology and development of Nassington.

Ryton Herb Gardens

Garden Organic, Coventry, Warwickshire CV8 3LG
Tel 024 7630 3517 www.hdra.org.uk

5 miles SE of Coventry off A45

Open all year, daily except Christmas week 9–5
Admission charge. Wheelchair access
Gift, food, wine shop; organic products
Owner Henry Doubleday Research Association

THE HERB GARDEN

Ryton is the home of the Henry Doubleday Research Association, the leading centre of organic gardening in the UK (recently renamed Garden Organic). There are 10 acres of landscaped gardens demonstrating all aspects of organic gardening from weed control and pest and disease control to reedbed sewage. There are fruit gardens and orchards, an allotment, a woodland walk, a wildflower meadow, all, of course rich in wild flowers, which are also herbs. This is also the home of the Heritage Seed Library which distributes to seeds that might otherwise disappear for ever. Free guided tours of the whole garden take place on Sat, Sun and Bank Holiday Mon at 11.30 and 2.30. The Herb Garden is a large circular area divided by paths into divisions of many species and cultivars. This is colourful at all times of year, not just in summer. For example in autumn as you enter the garden the startling orange and yellow leaves of *Rhus typhina* stand out against the silver and blue foliage of the Mediterranean herbs. The Paradise Garden, a memorial to the great gardener and TV presenter Geoff Hamilton, is full of colourful surprises. There is also a Rose Garden.

TEA

The restaurant, overlooking a floriferous patio, provides speciality teas and a wide range of herb teas, cream teas, cakes, scones and biscuits all made with organic ingredients, some grown in the garden. There are also tasty lunches served between 11−3.

Selsley Herb Nursery

Hayhedge Lane, Bisley, Stroud, Gloucestershire GL6 7AN
Tel 01452 770 073   www.selsleyherbs.co.uk

Off A419 to Sapperton, turn left just after Daneway pub through Waterlane, Nursery on right just before Bisley

Open Mar to Sep, Tue to Sat 10–5, Sun and bank holidays

2–5. Oct to Feb times variable, please phone
Admission free. Wheelchair access
Nursery; sale of English hand thrown terracotta pots
Owner Rob Wimperis

THE HERB GARDEN

Selsley Herb Nursery is a small specialist nursery offering a wide range of culinary, aromatic and medicinal herbs and other herbaceous plants. Previously set up by Rob's parents as Selsley Herb and Goat Farm at Selsley it moved in 2000 lock, stock (but not the goats) to its present site. The nursery itself is on the site of a former derelict nursery and is a lovely place with many established features such as beech hedges, trees, shrubs, roses and a magnificent pleached whitebeam hedge that forms the background to a new large display border. There are three new large knot gardens using different box varieties which are filled with culinary herbs.

TEA

Chancellor's Tea Room, Kingsley House, Victoria Street, Painswick (on the A46 Stroud–Cheltenham road on the corner past the churchyard) is a traditional tea room with home-made cakes, high teas, cream teas, scones as well as anything from savoury snacks to full roast dinners. Open Tues to Sun 10–5. Tel 01452 812451.

Shakespeare's Birthplace Gardens

Shakespeare Centre, Henley Street, Stratford-upon-Avon, Warwickshire CV37 6OW
Tel 01789 204016   www.shakespeare.org.uk
Open every day except Dec. Times vary, please phone
Admission charge. Wheelchair access
Visitor Centre; shops
Owner Shakespeare's Birthplace Trust

THE HERB GARDEN

The following four properties are all close to one another in Stratford-upon-Avon. They are cared for by the Shakespeare's Birthplace Trust and each of them has a garden that reflects the sort of plants that would have been grown in Shakespeare's time. There is a Visitor Centre

Shakespeare's Birthplace Garden, Henley Street

Entered through the Visitor Centre. This garden was bought for preservation as a national memorial to William Shakespeare in 1847. The garden layout has not been changed. You can wander down the paths and see herbs such as lavender, mints, savory and marjoram, neatly planted in semi-circles and well labelled. Trees associated with the period, such as a mulberry, quince and medlar, rub shoulders with a grape-vine, pomegranate and fig. Trees include cedar, oak, lime, hawthorn and silver birch. Of course, there are roses too (not always old roses).

The Great Garden, New Place, Chapel Street

This is the most beautiful and fascinating of the gardens and it is here that Shakespeare himself gardened and walked. Clipped, domed box hedges divide the borders into compartments containing such popular cottage garden flowers as hollyhocks, Canterbury bells, larkspurs and pansies. The wild bank has oxlips and eglantine, a wild rose similar to sweetbriar but with leaves that smell of apples when brushed. In the middle is an ancient mulberry tree, not the original but perhaps a cutting from that one. There is a knot garden, modelled on a pattern from Didymus Montaine's book *The Gardener's Labyrinth* published in 1577; and flower beds are edged with low-growing box filled with savory, hyssop, cotton lavender, thyme and other sweet-smelling traditional herbs. There is a shady tunnel of trees and crab apples. Limited wheelchair access.

Hall's Croft, Old Town

The home of Shakespeare's daughter Susanna and her husband Dr John Hall, this Tudor house is near the parish church where Shakespeare is buried. Here another mulberry shades the garden. There are shrub roses and cottage garden flowers in wide borders with quite a small but interesting plot of herbs grown by Dr Hall to help him treat his patients. He had a large practice and would have needed a great many herbs including those for his researches into scurvy. He discovered that fruit juices and herbs could help relieve the symptoms. Indoors you will find an Elizabethan dispensary with pestle and mortar, apothecaries' jars, dried herbs and herbal potions. Limited wheelchair access.

Anne Hathaway's Cottage, Shottery

One mile from Stratford town centre. This famous chocolate-box thatched cottage, where Shakespeare's wife Anne Hathaway lived before her marriage, presents the typical idea of a cottage garden of its day with a mixture of trees, shrubs, flowers and herbs all mingling together. Many pretty herbs can be seen including oxlips, pinks, milk thistles, foxgloves and mulleins. An orchard with old fruit trees is full of wild flowers in spring and summer. Ramped pathways.

TEA

Traditional cream teas are available for visitors to all the above gardens in the Visitor Centre and at some of the gardens as well.

Stockwood Craft Museum and Gardens

Farley Hill, Luton, Bedfordshire LU1 4BH
Tel 01582 738714

2 miles S of Luton town centre, close to Junction 10 of the M1

Open Apr to Oct Tue to Sat 10–5 Sun 10–6; Nov to Mar
Sat and Sun, Good Fri and Bank Holiday Mon 10–4
Admission free. Wheelchair access
Craft studios; museum of rural crafts and tools; antique
beehives
Owner Luton Museums Service

THE HERB GARDEN

The museum and gardens, opened officially in 1986,
are on the site of the former eighteenth-century
Stockwood House set in tranquil parkland. The
period gardens are in the original walled gardens of
the house, inspired by nine centuries of garden
history and include an Elizabeth kitchen garden and
a Victorian cottage garden, a sculpture garden, a
seventeenth-century Dutch garden featuring clipped
hedges and urns, replicating the design by William
Kent for Alexander Pope's garden in Twickenham.
The Medieval Garden (twelfth to fifteenth centuries)
shows herbs and plants grown for medicinal use,
cooking and dyeing. The sixteenth-century garden is
laid out in knots, a favourite feature of Elizabethan
gardens. It has been planted with traditional herbs
such as germander, hyssop and box, with the open
areas filled with brick dust or powdered shells to
contrast with the greenery.

TEA

The tearooms in the old stables serve teas and also
serve light refreshments.

Toddington Manor

Toddington, Bedfordshire LU5 6HJ
Tel 01525 872576

Signed from Toddington village

Open Jun and Jul: pre-booked visits
Owner Sir Nevile and Lady Bowman-Shaw

THE HERB GARDEN

The original gardens were destroyed many years ago; only a few mature trees have survived. The present owners began replanting in 1979 and the gardens are improving year by year. There is a lime (*Tilia platyphyllus*) avenue casting heavy shadow over hellebores, ferns, hostas, bluebells and other shade loving plants. This leads to a cherry walk and there are walks through woods and by lakes. The magnificent long herbaceous borders are 6m wide divided by a wide central path. The Herb Garden itself was planted in 1968 to a design by Lucy Huntington. It is protected on two sides by the old kitchen garden wall. The outer border has plants to reflect the culinary, medicinal and insect repellent virtues of the herbs. The inner section is planted with some of the many species and cultivars of thyme. The Rose Garden was reconstructed in the 1970s with a central fish pond. There are diagonally symmetrical white 'Iceberg' floribunda roses in opposite corners. These have recently been underplanted with woodruff (*Galium odorata*), heartsease (*Viola tricolor*) and snow-in-summer (*Cerastium tomentosum*). The Swimming Pool Garden is an unusually charming setting for a refreshing dip in the pool and provides evergreen structure with colour right through summer provided by delphiniums, lavender, rue and rosemary. George's Bed supports old-fashioned roses on poles and chains including 'Félicité Perpétue' and 'Mme Alfred Carrière' associated with many peonies and foxgloves.

TEA

There are no facilities for tea at Toddington but The Poplars Nursery Garden Centre, Harlington Road, Toddington has a large tea shop/restaurant within the nursery with good chocolate fudge brownies, among other treats.

Victorian Chemist Shop & Physic Garden

Hitchin Museum, Paynes Park, Hitchin, Herts SG5 1EW
Tel 01462 434476   www.nhdc.gov.uk

In the centre of Hitchin where the A505 and the A602 meet

Open Mon to Sat, except public holidays
Admission free. Wheelchair access
Recreation of chemist's shop (plus many other displays on local industries and domestic life); art gallery
Owner Hertfordshire Medical and Pharmaceutical Museum Trust

The Hitchin chemist Perks & Llewellyn ceased trading in 1961. The last pharmacist, Miss V E Lewis bought much of the stock and fittings of the High Street pharmacy and the reconstructed shop was open by appointment in her own house. But she wanted her collection to be enjoyed by a wider audience and donated it to the Hertfordshire Medical and Pharmaceutical Museum trust where the collection now has its permanent home with an evocative re-creation of the chemists' shop complete with mahogany fittings and colourful bottles. Original cabinets contain the lavender toiletries for which Perks & Llwellyn were famed worldwide. Display panels and an interactive computer interpret the collection and describe the growing and processing of the lavender (grown nearby for 400 years) from which Hitchin became known as 'Lavender Town'.

THE HERB GARDEN

The small Physic Garden reflects the historical and modern importance of medicinal plants. It has a central sculpture in the form of a pestle and mortar standing on a cobbled circle and surrounded by a series of stone slab paths and benches from which you can enjoy the beds of many medicinal plants in which lavender features strongly. The garden also celebrates the production of plant-based drugs by

William Ransom & Son, manufacturing chemists in
Hitchin for over 140 years.

Hidden extra: Cadwell Farm at nearby Ickleford
started growing twelve acres of lavender and some of
flax about five years ago. The field has a footpath
alongside it reached from Ickleford via the Icknield
Way or from the Willbury Hills picnic site on the
Stotfold road. June and July are the times to visit
and the farm arranges lavender walks during those
months. Tel 01462 434320
www.HitchinLavender.com.

TEA

The museum has no café but the High Street and
Market Place are full of coffee shops such as Café
Nero and Café Rouge and places to snack or eat
seriously.

Waltham Place

Church Hill, White Waltham, Maidenhead, Berkshire SL6
3JH
Tel 01628 825517   walthamplace.org.uk

*3¹/2 miles S of Maidenhead, Junction 8/9 of M4, then A404
In White Waltham turn left at St Mary's Church. Parking
signed at top of hill*

Open Apr to Sep weekdays 10-4
Admission charge; limited wheelchair access
Farm shop with organic produce
Owner Lady Oppenheimer

THE HERB GARDEN

Waltham Place has 170 acres of extensive landscape
and ornamental gardens all run according to organic
principles. The present design of the gardens is the
result of a visit by Lady Oppenheimer to Priona
Gardens of Henk Gerritsen in Holland in 1999.
Plants and many herbs are seen with a rather
different eye, accepting a less formal, less tidy

appearance as a result of adapting plants to the ecology of the place rather than producing a formal decorative garden. There's a series of walled gardens, the oldest from the seventeenth century, an English landscape garden with splendid specimen trees, a huge double border enclosed by yew hedge and many intimate areas. The Herb Garden itself is a small paved area with a backdrop of mature Banksia roses. This garden is still being developed and may end up as a biblical garden with plants actually mentioned in the Bible. The Butterfly Garden is a tiny space surrounded by tall hedges and an arch, full of perennials and self-seeding annuals. The Friars' Walk is a long, narrow walled garden planted with hot colours counterbalanced by brown, orange, grey and greenish yellow. Euphorbias, bronze fennel, artemisias and grasses help to subdue the tone. The Square Garden is almost an acre in size. A giant caterpillar of clipped box interconnects both halves of the garden and also acts as a frame to the surrounding planting. On the caterpillar's south are tall and rugged plants chosen for their ability to compete with indigenous weeds such as ground elder and partly to juxtapose with smaller gravel plants.

TEA

The gracious old barn was refurbished in 2003 to house the shop and tea room where you can get delicious home-made cakes and biscuits, all of organically produced ingredients.

EAST ANGLIA

Norfolk Lavender •

• Felbrigg Hall

KINGS LYNN ●

Castle Acre
Priory
●•

● SWAFFHAM

NORWICH

●

• Oxburgh Hall
Laurel Farm Herbs •

CAMBRIDGE ●• • Cambridge University Botanic Gdn

Emmanuel College

BURY ●
ST EDMUNDS

• Netherfield Herbs

IPSWICH

Tudor Herb Garden •

BRAINTREE ●

Knights Templar Garden •

Helmingham
Hall

LONDON

The sites of the gardens shown on
this map are approximate. They will give
an indication as to how you might plan
your visits. For precise instructions on
finding the gardens, please refer to the
specific information for each garden.

Cambridge University Botanic Garden

Bateman Street, Cambridge CB2 1JF
Tel 01223 336265   www.botanic.cam.ac.uk

3/4 of a mile South of the city centre by Trumpington Road (A10)

Open daily summer 10–6; (5 in spring and autumn 4 in winter); closed 25 Dec to 5 Jan
Admission charge. Wheelchair access.
Shop
Owner Cambridge University

The botanic garden was established in 1761 for teaching botany and science. Today plants are grown for scientific research in a garden for visitors to enjoy and learn from. This garden is beautiful in all seasons with a spectacular winter garden bursting with colour in the gloomiest part of the year. It holds the National Collections of Saxifrages and Geraniums.

THE HERB GARDEN

There is a chronological border containing a selection of plants introduced into Britain from earliest times. Many of these are herbs. You will find the saffron crocus, rosemary, *Nicotiana tabascum* (brought over from the New World in 1586), nasturtiums from Peru, bergamot (first grown in Britain from seed sent by the American botanist John Bartram). The systematic or 'order' beds are referred to as 'herb borders'. These are large informal beds, each devoted to a specific family and informatively labelled. The area is divided by the occasional clipped hawthorn hedge. Here you will find many unusual and fascinating plants including the black pea, black medick, strawberry clover, hog's fennel, shrubby hare's ear, wild rue, mandrake, *Vitis agnus-castus*, jimson weed with cherry tomatoes growing amongst it, and so much more. The scented garden contains heliotrope, pelargoniums, mint, pinks, thymes, rosemary and scented roses and rue in a semi circular bed where scents can hang in the atmosphere. In the rose garden eight beds tell the history of roses from the apothecary's rose to today's floribundas. There is plenty to keep you entertained for a day and plenty of benches to sit on too.

TEA

In the Gilmour Building the Cambridge Coffee Company offers a selection of teas including herbal teas, cream teas and a good selection of cakes, buns and scones, coffee, hot chocolate and ice cream to eat indoors or out.

Castle Acre Priory

Castle Acre, nr Swaffham, Norfolk PE32 2AJ
Tel 01760 755394

1/2 mile W of the village of Castle Acre, 5 miles N of Swaffham

Open Apr to Sep daily 10–6; Oct daily 10–5; Nov to Mar Wed to Sun 10–4. Closed for lunch 1–2
Admission charge (EH members free). Wheelchair access to grounds
Gift shop; museum
Owner English Heritage

The priory was built in 1090, inspired by the Abbey of Cluny in Burgundy. In 1537 it was surrendered to Henry VIII during the Dissolution of the Monasteries.

THE HERB GARDEN

There is a deceptively small re-created walled herb garden next to the visitor centre. Herbs are grown here in 24 large rectangular beds (measuring about 1m x 1¹/2 metres) set amongst brick paths with more beds round the walls. Groups of beds are dedicated to herbs for different uses. Healing plants include comfrey, wall germander, fennel, lady's mantle, peony, bugle, pennyroyal and golden sage. Culinary herbs include borage, parsley, welsh onion, chives, various mints, thyme, common sage and rosemary. Decorative and dyeing herbs include St John's wort, curry plant, southernwood, lavender, Roman chamomile, woad and lemon balm. Strewing herbs include tansy, hyssop, lavender, rosemary, cotton lavender and woodruff. There are cordoned apples along one wall, clipped box shapes, the apothecary's rose, sweet violets, snowdrops, wild strawberries, feverfew, honeysuckle and more including many scented plants. The herbs are those that the monks would have grown and used for everyday purposes and are well labelled.

TEA

There are no teas at the priory but Willow Cottage, Stocks Green, Castle Acre (Tel 01760 755551) has a charming tea room with pretty table cloths and china where you can get a pot of tea or fresh filter coffee. There's a really scrumptious choice of home made cake, gateaux and tea breads, or a Norfolk cream tea with freshly baked scones plus ice creams.

Emmanuel College Herb Garden

Emmanuel College, University of Cambridge, St Andrew's Street, Cambridge CB2 3AP   Tel 01223 334200
Open daily 9–5
Admission free. Wheelchair access
Owner the Master, Fellows and Scholars of Emmanuel College

THE HERB GARDEN

In New Court is a large and formal herb garden designed by John Codrington in 1961, a nod perhaps to the Dominican priory which held the land before the college took it over after the Reformation. It is as interesting architecturally, perhaps as botanically, being designed to fit in with the patterns of student movements from one part of the college to another.

The strictly geometrical layout includes wide York stone paths bordered with brick and cobblestones. The garden is based on an early seventeenth-century design. The three triangular beds are surrounded by box hedges broken up into a number of small plots interlaced with more box hedges. Each space is planted with a single herb species, chosen largely for their ornamental foliage making interesting contrasts of texture. Coloured chippings are also added to provide contrasts of colour. Among the rosemaries, thymes, hyssop and lemon balm are some more unusual herbs such as dwarf white lavender, sweet Cicely and elecampane. Height is added by introducing clipped bay trees. Along the walls are scented shrubs and climbing roses including the very thorny Scotch rose *Rosa spinosissima*, *Rosa* 'Crimson Glory' and tree germander *Teucrium fruticans*.

TEA

Auntie's Tea Shop, 1 St Mary's Passage, Cambridge has two rooms and is always busy. It has a range of ten teas and fruit and herbal teas served by waitresses in traditional black and white uniforms, fresh baked cakes, éclairs, cream teas and egg-and-cress sandwiches. Open summer Mon to Sat 7.30–6 (winter to 5.30) Sun 1–5.30. Tel 01223 315641.

Felbrigg Hall Herb Garden

Felbrigg Hall, Norwich, Norfolk NR11 8PR
Tel 01263 837 444

Near Felbrigg village 2 miles SW of Cromer off B1436, signposted from A148 and A140

Open early Apr to late Oct Mon to Wed 10–5; Sat and Sun 11–5 Admission charge (NT members free). Largely accessible to wheelchairs
Shop; second-hand bookshop; plant sales
Owner The National Trust

This fine seventeenth-century house contains its original eighteenth-century furniture. The park contains an orangery and well-preserved woodlands.

THE HERB GARDEN

A short walk through the park leads to the large and beatiful Walled Garden. Work on restoring this garden started in 1972 and the result is spectacularly pleasing. The design features a series of *potager* gardens, a very attractive working dovecote and the National Collection of *Colchicums*. From the moment you enter you are captivated by the originality of the planting and the quality of the plants. Clipped box hedges carry the eye along generous paths and fascinating borders. The central path delights the eye with bright floral beds on either side. Turn left and you will come to the herb border which runs the whole length of one wall. But there are herbs throughout the garden and many unusual plants. Herbs grown include golden sage, lavender, cotton lavender, rosemary, lovage and many other Mediterranean-style herbs that do well in this sandy soil. There are plenty of seats for leisurely enjoyment of the garden. One wall has golden roses climbing to the top spectacularly interspersed with blue ceanothus (Californian lilac). Fruit trees are trained along the red brick walls. I visited the garden in pouring rain and was still enchanted.

TEA

The licensed Turret Restaurant is in the stable courtyard and offers a selection of teas (including orange and lotus flower, blackcurrant, peppermint, raspberry and elderflower) plus a really sharp ginger beer and home-made cakes. There is also a separate tea room, a bit more basic but with much the same choice of teas and there are picnic tables in the car park.

Helmingham Hall Herb Garden

Helmingham Hall Gardens, Helmingham, Stowmarket,
Suffolk IP14 6EF   Tel 01473 890 363
www.helminghamestate.com

*9 miles N of Ipswich on the B1077; 3 miles S of
Stowmarket/Yoxford Road (A1120)*

Open early May to early Sep, every Sun 2–6
Admission charge. Wheelchair access
Shop with gifts and Helmingham produce
Owner Lord Tollemache

Helmingham Hall is a stately red brick Tudor
mansion set in beautiful parkland with red deer. It
has been the home of the Tollemache family for 500
years. The garden moat is probably of Saxon origin.
The Victorian garden leads to a walled Elizabethan
kitchen garden surrounded by a Saxon moat. Here
are meticulously maintained herbaceous borders,
old-fashioned roses surrounded by vegetable beds,
tunnels of sweet peas, runner beans and gourds.

THE HERB GARDEN

The hybrid musk rose garden was redesigned in 1965
by Dinah Lady Tollemache. Lady Xa Tollemache,
wife of the present owner, has designed a second
rose garden, a knot garden, the large and wonderful
walled garden and the herb garden. On the east side
of the Hall the historic herb and knot garden has a
magnificent collection of shrub roses. These gardens
are divided into shaped beds with grass walks
between them, surrounded by clipped yew hedges
with openings leading into other areas of the garden.
All the plants are contemporary with the house.

TEA

Cream teas are available in the Old Coach House
with home-made cakes, scones and sandwiches.
There is also a picnic area.

Knights Templar Garden

Cressing Temple, Witham Road, Braintree, Essex CM7 8PD   Tel 01376 584903

3 miles N of Witham on the B1018; from A12 follow brown signs to Freeport until you see Cressing Temple's own brown sign

Open Mar to Oct Sun 10.30–5; May to Sep Wed, Thur, Fri 10.30–4.30. At other times please call for appointment Admission charge. Wheelchair access to ground floor and garden. No dogs
Owner Essex County Council

Cressing Temple is dominated by two huge thirteenth-century barns originally commissioned by the Knights Templar. In the wheat barn is an exhibition exploring the history of Cressing Temple. There is also the Elizabethan granary, an eighteenth-century cart-lodge, a wheelwright's shop, a nineteenth-century bakehouse and a twentieth-century well-house.

THE HERB GARDEN

The original walled garden was built in the sixteenth century as a formal pleasure garden at the rear of the Great House that once stood here. Substantial areas of the original walls remain and archaeological excavations have revealed brick walls to a viewing terrace which ran along the eastern side of the garden. There is also some Tudor brick paving. These features are incorporated in today's garden but there is not enough evidence for a full reconstruction so instead painstaking research using paintings, woodcuts and documents has allowed a garden to be recreated in a style faithful to the original designs of the period. The planting echoes this. All the plants used in the garden would have been available in the sixteenth and seventeenth centuries including the now rare bee orchid. The site is also rich in wildlife, so take your binoculars!

TEA

Cressing Temple has its own restaurant with tea, coffee, cream teas and a delicious range of tempting cakes and sandwiches, also light lunches.

Laurel Farm Herbs

Saxmundham, Suffolk IP17 2RG   Tel 01728 668 223

On the A12 two miles S of Saxmundham

Open during nursery opening times.
Admission free. Wheelchair access
Nursery
Owner Chris Seagon

THE HERB GARDEN

The demonstration garden attached to this nursery is on a very exposed site and has much of interest. It has recently been redesigned and replanted in an informal circular shape with gravel paths and surrounding beds. All beds are raised, including a raised brick bed and other separate raised beds of timber to alleviate the heavy clay soil. Some of the original plants have been reinstated including a *Myrtus communis*. This alone, growing in heavy clay and in full wind proves it is hardier than people think and the books say – worth a visit for this plant alone. There is also a newly planted bog garden full of culinary and medicinal plants that cope with damp soils.

TEA

Weavers Tea Room, 2 The Knoll, Peasenhall, Saxmundham is a pretty little tea room with speciality teas including Assam, Lapsang Souchong, Darjeeling and herbal teas plus cream teas and a good range of home-cooked meals. Closed Wed. Tel 01728 660548.

Netherfield Herbs

The Thatched Cottage, 37 Nether Street, Rougham, Suffolk
IP30 9LW   Tel 01359 270452

*About half way between Bury St Edmunds and Woolpit off
the A14*

Open informally most days. Please telephone first
Wheelchair access difficult because of grass paths
Owner Lesley Bremness

THE HERB GARDEN

This private herb garden is a perfect foil for its
chocolate-box thatched cottage. It is based on
Lesley's winning design as Herb Garden of the Year
in a competition organised by the Herb Society and
Garden News. It is a series of interlocking squares
with brick and grass paths. A scented arbour
surrounds a seat and raised sink gardens display
dwarf herbs. There are masses of well-known and
well-loved herbs such as varieties of thyme,
marjoram and mint. Unusual herbs include a pink
rosemary, a dwarf curry plant, a prostrate winter
savory and a variegated rue. Lesley is an avid plant
collector, a garden designer (she designed the first
Herb Society garden at the Chelsea Flower Show)
and a successful author. Her enthusiasm and
curiosity for new ideas means the garden is
constantly evolving and changing and always has
interesting things to look at and enjoy.

TEA

No teas at the garden but The Kitchen Garden,
Church Cottage, Troston, Bury St Edmunds IP31 1EX
is only about 15 minutes away and serves tea (a
selection of herb teas if you like) and home-made
cakes on Fri to Sat from Easter to end Sept 10–5.
Tel 01359 268322. (The owner, Francine Raymond is
a hen specialist and has a shop selling books, cards
and gifts related to hens and gardens).

Norfolk Lavender

Caley Mill, Heacham, Kings Lynn, Norfolk PE31 7JE
Tel 01485 571176   admin@norfolk-lavender.co.uk
www.norfolk-lavender.co.uk

Take A1478 from Kings Lynn or Hunstanton or B1484 from Norwich

Open Nov to Mar 10–4. Apr to Oct 10–5
Admission charge. Wheelchair access
Shops; plants; children's play centre; tours of gardens and lavender fields
Owners The Head family

Caley Mill is a nineteenth-century water mill, now the site of a well-known lavender farm growing perfume grade English lavender and also distilling lavender on site. You can take a minibus trip to the 50 acre lavender fields and see the National Collection of Lavenders. Everything is grown without pesticides. There is also a fragrant meadow garden.

THE HERB GARDEN

The herb garden, the first thing you approach from the car park, has more than 55 individual brick-edged beds of labelled herbs set out in the style of an old monastery herb garden with wide brick paths, wooden benches and a locally made sundial in the centre. Through an archway is the newly planted lavender garden where visitors can sit under a pergola and enjoy the new vistas and many different lavender varieties. Most of the plants grown are available at the plant centre and conservatory shop. Dried lavender flowers are used in many of the products on sale.

TEA

The spacious Norfolk Lavender self-service café/tea room in the converted miller's cottage can seat about 120 people and offers a relaxing environment with a log fire in winter and patio seating in summer. It provides various teas, herbal teas and coffee, cream teas, and home-made lavender scones and

cakes as well as snacks, sandwiches and a selection
of hot dishes.

Old Hall Plants

1 The Old Hall, Barsham, Beccles, Suffolk NR34 8HB
Tel 01502 717 475   www.oldhallplants.freeserve.co.uk

Off the B1062 between Beccles and Bungay

Open most days by appointment
Admission free. Poor wheelchair access
Nursery
Owner Janet Elliott

THE HERB GARDEN

The nursery is an organic smallholding, about 1/3
acre, set around the recently restored manor house
built in the fifteenth century by Sir John Suckley,
Secretary of State to James I. Janet Elliott grows 600
species of herbs, all propagated on site, some
extremely rare originating from all over the world.
Some have Aztec connections, others Australian
Aborigine or American Indian connections. Some are
from the Far East and others from the
Mediterranean. All are propagated on site. For £14
you can take a tour of the Old Hall, Barsham Church
and the nursery with wine and a buffet lunch.

TEA

No teas at the nursery, but Winter Flora Centre for
Unusual Plants, Hall Farm, London Road, Beccles
(just down the road) offers good teas, has a pleasant
garden and sells dried and silk flowers. Tel 01502
713346. Or The Flying Fifteens, 19a The Esplanade,
Lowestoft (about 8 miles away) overlooking the sea
offers 26 special teas including Good Luck Green Tea
in china pots with a mouth-watering choice of cakes
including meringues, sponges and strawberry scones,
as well as savouries and soups. Open Tues to Sun
10.30–4.30. Closed winter. Tel 01502 581 188.

Oxburgh Hall

Oxborough, Kings Lynn, PE33 9PS   Tel 01366 328258

In Oxborough, 9 miles E of Downham Market by A1122 and A134

Open most of the year but opening times vary so please telephone first
Admission charge (NT members free). Recommended route for wheelchairs (care necessary near moat)
NT shop; second-hand bookshop during the season
Owners The National Trust

Beautifully proportioned Elizabethan house on the edge of a small Norfolk village with a wide moat and a ha ha on two sides. In the nineteenth century the owners, a family called Bedingfield, visited France and were impressed by the French parterres they saw in Paris and the parterre next to the house was inspired by what they saw. Although owned by the National Trust members of the family still live in the hall.

THE HERB GARDENS

Although there is no herb garden as such, Oxburgh Hall is rich in herbs mainly culinary and as decorative plants in the garden. The parterres are of intricate design with box-edged scrolls filled with permanent plantings of rue and santolina plus summer bedding of ageratums, marigolds and pelargoniums. When the National Trust restored this garden traces of the coal and cement originally used to fill the spaces with colour were clearly visible.
A long herbaceous border is separated from the parterre by a clipped yew hedge and is bordered by a long 'hedge' of catmint lavender. The walled kitchen garden encloses an orchard of medlars and mulberries and an attractive and productive potager. The orchard's 100 year old yew hedge (yew is used in the treatment of some cancers) is being regenerated. It was cut practically back to the ground on one side in January 2005 and the other side in August (so as

not to give it too great a shock), fed, mulched and watered and regrowth is already strong and healthy. The orchard walls are buttressed by clipped bay at regular intervals. The potager beds are bordered by tiny clipped box hedges. There is a bed of culinary herbs and others are grown round the greenhouse. These include chives, garlic chives, parsley, mint, sage, marjoram. Elsewhere are huge clumps of cotton lavender and lovage. Both vegetables and herbs are used in the kitchen.

T E A

There is a licensed restaurant in the Old Kitchen selling good National Trust fare including home made cakes, a selection of teas including vanilla, lemon and ginger and raspberry leaf, and soups and slalads made with produce from the potager. Some dishes are relevant to Tudor times – modified for today. There are picnic tables in the car park and woodlands and you can get ice creams at the entrance.

Tudor Herb Garden

Kentwell Hall, Long Melford, Suffolk CO1D 9BA
Tel 01787 310207   www.kentwellhall.co.uk

Off the A134 between Bury St Edmunds and Sudbury

Open times vary, please phone or check on website
Admission charge. Wheelchair access to most of grounds
Farm; tours of house
Owner Patrick Phillips

Kentwell Hall describes itself as 'not a stately home as is generally understood – certainly its occupants are not stately. It is very much a lived-in and loved famil home, something it has been for over 500 years.' You approach it by a three-quarter mile long ancient lime avenue leading to its mellow soft red brickwork and broad moats. The gardens at Kentwell Hall are a combination of ancient features, elements

of alterations made by Lady Guthrie who lived here
during the 1930s and recent landscaping and
planting by the Phillips. There is a shrubbery, a
sunken garden, tennis court, thujas and a herbaceous
border planted in rainbow colours. In front of the
house are lawns, a ha-ha and a large wildlife pond. A
circle of mature oaks was planted for the Queen's
Jubilee and there is a sixteenth-century cottage
garden. Other attractions are animals, fish in the
pond and peacocks. Particularly unusual are the two
dimensional brick maze, which is both unusual and a
puzzle, laid out by Judith Phillips. It is based on a
Tudor rose and incorporates various Tudor symbols.

THE HERB GARDENS

The walled garden retains vestiges of the sixteenth
century in its irregular shape and some of its wall
but more of the seventeenth century (espaliered fruit
trees, layout and other parts of the wall). Both
periods have been accentuated by the recent addition
of a large specific herb garden and a potager laid out
with paths and some old roses. This is very peaceful
and sheltered – a lovely place to walk in and try to
identify the plants. It is cared for by a local doctor
and sometimes could do with a bit of a haircut but is
well worth a visit. The herbs are not individually
labelled but there is a comprehensive label at the
entrance telling what may be found, divided into
culinary and medicinal herbs. More unusual herbs
include skirret, agrimony, nonesuch, woad,
elecampsia, southernwood, alecost, tansy, self heal,
orris, dyeplaxis and woodruff. The many ancient
yews, some 50ft tall, are being clipped into shape;
cedars exist from the eighteenth century when the
moat was enlarged. A wild bank grows wild orchids.

TEA

There are three restaurants but some are only open
for special occasions, so please phone to check which
restaurants are open (01787 310207). In the
Undercroft you can get teas and light lunches in the

space under the east wing of the house with a splendid mural on the walls; the Stableyard Kitchen serves hot and cold drinks, chips and burgers; the Spit Roast operates on special days.

NORTH
OF
ENGLAND

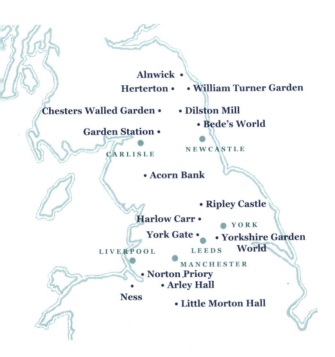

The sites of the gardens shown on this map are approximate. They will give an indication as to how you might plan your visits. For precise instructions on finding the gardens, please refer to the specific information for each garden.

Acorn Bank Herb Garden

Acorn Bank Garden and Watermill, Temple Sowerby,
Nr Penrith, Cumbria CA10 1SP
Tel 01768 361467

Just N of Temple Sowerby, 6 miles E of Penrith on A66

Open late Mar to late Oct daily (except Tue) 10–5
Admission charge (NT members free). Wheelchair access
NT shop; plant sales
Owner The National Trust

THE HERB GARDENS

Delightful sheltered garden protected from the
Cumbrian climate by ancient oaks and high enclosing
brick walls, and renowned for its herbs and orchards
growing old English fruit varieties. On the north are
extensive views over open country.

The garden runs from east to west and contains a
long middle bed with wide borders running down
each side finishing in a holly hedge. Shade-loving
herbs are grown under trees, Mediterranean-type
plants in more open areas. There are 240 or so
plants growing here. These include marsh mallow,
mountain spinach with deep red leaves, giant
elecampane, monkshood, bergamot, and many more.

TEA

There is a restaurant serving the usual good NT fare
where you can get teas, scones and cakes.

Alnwick Poisonous Garden

Denwick Lane, Alnwick, NE66 1YU
Tel 01665 511350   www.alnwickgarden.com

Signed in Alnwick and from the A1

Open daily except Christmas Day 10–5
Admission charge; car parking charge. Wheelchair access
Gift shop
Owner Alnwick Garden Enterprises

The Alnwick Garden is that unusual thing, a privately created twentieth-century grand garden in the spirit of eighteenth- and nineteenth-century stately gardens – designed for the general public. Designed by Belgian garden designer Jacques Wirtz, with his son Peter, for the Duchess of Northumberland, it has been many years under construction and opened to the public in 2001. The main feature is a water cascade flanked by hornbeam arcades. There are many other gardens to provide interest throughout the year. These include a Rose Garden with 3,000 roses from David Austin including the Alnwick Rose (launched 2001), the Ornamental Garden, the Woodland Walk, the Serpentine Garden full of water sculptures within clipped yew hedges and the Bamboo Labyrinth. The Garden is continually evolving and there are plants for a Quiet Garden, amongst others.

THE POISONOUS GARDEN

The Poisonous Garden was opened for the first time in Autumn 2004 and is still settling in. You enter this asymmetrical garden through ivy-curtained tunnels. Garden Consultant Caroline Holmes selected the plants to fit in with Peter Wirtz's design of flame-shaped beds (some kept behind bars for safety reasons). Your Guide will unlock the wrought iron gate to let you in then take you round the beds and point out particular plants, explaining their history and uses in an entertaining and informative way. Home Office approval has been obtained to grow cannabis and magic mushrooms, but there are also many traditional killers and cures such as hemlock, digitalis, nicotiana, and many more. Special cloches have been created to provide a micro-climate for the plants.

TEA

The Garden Café is set within the garden with views over the Grand cascade and serves local produce including home-made cakes, scones and biscuits.

The Tree House Café is in the extraordinary tree house – well, more of a tree village – and offers home-made Northumbrian fare.

Arley Hall Herb Garden

Arley Hall and Gardens, Great Budworth, Northwich, Cheshire CW9 6NA

Tel 01565 777353   www.arleyhallandgardens.com

10 min from Junction 20 of the M6 or Junction 10 of the M56 approx 6 miles from High Leigh

Open late Mar to late Sep (and weekends in Oct) Tue to Sun and Bank Holiday Mon 11–5
Admission charge. Wheelchair access
Gift shop; plant nursery
Owner Viscount and Viscountess Ashbrook

This fascinating combination of ancient buildings and comparatively modern but quintessentially English garden is still a family home. The gardens, lovingly created by successive generations of the same family since the nineteenth century, include a spectacular double herbaceous border supposed to be the oldest in England. The Flag Garden (referring to the stone flagged paths) is planted with roses, dwarf lavender and other summer flowering plants.

THE HERB GARDEN

The herb garden started out as a compost tip from the large kitchen garden during WW2 and later became a market garden. In 1968 it was turned into a garden of herbs and useful or scented plants. It has an interesting formal shape made up of ten rectangular plots divided by paths of paving setts and gravel. The herbs, largely culinary or designed to give pleasure to garden visitors, include rosemary, rue, sages, angelica, lovage and chives, thymes of various kinds, and mints, and hyssop, bergamot, fennel, vervain, sorrel and tree onions. A neighbouring scented garden, made in 1977, is planted with aromatic shrubs and flowers in a series of raised beds of irregular shapes.

TEA

Teas are available in the converted Tudor barn furnished with antique chairs and oak tables. Here you can get dainty sandwiches followed by home-made tea bread with lemon curd, or cake. There are home-made scones with strawberry jam and home-made ice-cream, all very much in keeping with the elegant setting. You can also get light refreshments.

Bede's World Herb Garden

Bede's World, Church Bank, Jarrow NE32 3DY.
Tel 0191 489 2106   www.bedesworld.co.uk

2 miles from the A18 Tyne Tunnel (toll tunnel), south entrance

Open daily 10–5.30, Sun from 12.30, Nov to Mar closes 4.30. Garden only free. Wheelchair access
Herbal gift shop, sales of local crafts, bookshop
Owner Bede's World

The Anglo-Saxon Monastery of St Paul's was founded in 681 AD. It is now run by an educational charity with an Anglo-Saxon farm and vegetable garden where early cultivars of vegetables are grown. There is also an interesting herb garden.

THE HERB GARDEN

The garden was initially designed by Rosemary Cramp and Richard Kilburn in 1978 and is now maintained by a team of volunteers who can be seen working the garden most Thursday mornings. The first part of the garden, as you enter, draws on the structure of a typical medieval *physick* garden with trellis work and a central arch marking the entrance, leading to four oblong beds, two on either side of a central aisle. The first two of these beds contain herbs from the Anglo-Saxon age; behind these are a bed of culinary herbs and one of medicinal herbs. The second part of the garden is based on the ninth-century plan of the Monastery of St Gall in Switzerland, showing the ecclesiastical and domestic buildings. Plans for two large gardens, one for medicinal and one for culinary herbs, survive on this plan and there was also an orchard. The long, narrow rectangular beds at Bede's are based on those shown on the St Gall plan, although the planting is not replicated exactly – here plants are based on Anglo-Saxon and medieval varieties suitable for the local soil and climate.

TEA

The Jarrow Hall Café is a stylish restaurant offering a wide selection of coffees, teas, herbal teas and hot chocolate alongside home baked scones, pastries, cakes and cream gateaux, as well as sandwiches, soup and salads, all freshly made to order.

Chesters Walled Garden

(previously known as Hexham Herbs)
Chollerford, Hexham, Northumberland NE46 4BQ.
Tel 01434 681483   www.chesterswalledgarden.co.uk

6 miles N of Hexham, just off the B6318, known locally as the 'Military Road' and half a mile west of Chollerford

Open Apr to Oct 10–5; Nov to Mar depends on the weather, please phone first
Small entrance charge to garden and woodland walk.
Wheelchair access
Nursery; shop
Owner Mrs S White

THE HERB GARDEN

Chesters Walled Garden is a 2-acre eighteenth-century garden, originally the fruit and vegetable garden for Chesters House. The garden has now been laid out as a unique herb and herbaceous garden with one of the largest collections of herbs in the country, and is grown entirely organically and in a way to attract wildlife. Wildflowers are woven in amongst the rarer perennials in an informal mix which is particularly attractive. This gives a loose, relaxed style of planting and gives plenty of nectar for native insects. There are wide gravel paths, espalier apple trees, clipped box hedges and long vistas. Chesters holds the National Thyme Collection growing on a 30m raised bank, at its peak in June and July when it resembles a Persian carpet of glowing colours and is alive with bees. A fine Mediterranean Border of rosemaries, sages and other highly scented herbs growing in gravel also houses the National Collection of Marjoram. There are reflective pools and a fountain. The Roman Garden displays culinary, medicinal and sacred plants laid out in small formal beds. In the Walled Garden the 400 or so varieties of roses, grown for their scent, are at their peak in July. There are extensive herbaceous borders and a medieval box knot garden planted to a design of 1617.

TEA

The nursery does not provide teas but in the pretty village of Simonburn you can get teas in the Blackhall Tea Room, The Mains and sit in the garden. There are also cafés, restaurants and pubs in Hexham such as Athena's Restaurant, 10 Hallgate, offering home-baked dishes (including vegetarian and Mediterranean) from local outlets.

Dilston Physic Garden

Dilston Mill House, near Corbridge, Northumberland NE45 5QZ
Contact Johanna Sheehan 01434 606159,
Katrina Padmore 01434 873593 or
Elaine Perry: e.k.perry@ncl.uk

About 2 miles from Hexham and 1 mile from Corbridge on A695 turn off along lane marked 'Dilston Mill B&B'

Open Apr to Sep Wed 10–12 noon (weather permitting)
Admission charge. Not accessible to wheelchairs
Plants for sale
Owner Prof. Elaine Perry

THE HERB GARDEN

Professor Perry is a neuroscientist and Director of the Medicinal Plant Research Centre at the University of Newcastle. She has created this spectacular botanic garden on a hill, partly to provide herbs for her research at the university. It has over 500 medicinal herbs each clearly labelled with its Latin name and traditional uses, updated with new scientific and clinical evidence. The garden meanders in informal paths giving spectacular views over the beautiful Tyne valley. It includes a Chamomile Lawn, a Sage Garden, a Bamboo Avenue and a Poison Garden and has a spectacular bright red Chinese gate. Courses are available on such subjects as medical herbalism, aromatherapy, flower essences, plants of the gods and astrological aspects.

TEA

Freshly made teas from herbs in the garden are available on request during visits to the garden.

The Garden Station

Langley-on-Tyne, Hexham, Northumberland NE47 5LA
Tel 01434 684391   www.thegardenstation.co.uk

Take the A686 turning off the A69 Newcastle to Carlisle road at Haydon Bridge. Continue for 2^1/$_2$ miles then follow yellow signs to left just past Langley sawmill

Open May to Aug, Tue to Sun and bank holidays 10–5
Admission free. Wheelchair access
Plants for sale
Owner Jane Torday

THE HERB GARDEN

Sheltered by ancient woodland, The Garden Station

is a very pretty restored Victorian railway station which was closed in 1950 and reincarnated in 2000 as a centre for gardening and art courses. A tranquil garden full of woodland plants has been developed along the old railway line leading away under stone-arched bridges into the wilder woodland beyond. The garden around the station itself is south facing and aromatic herbs thrive here in the sun. A few minutes walk away is the new Garden Station vegetable allotment where, by midsummer, herb spirals make ornamental mounds of flowers and scent. A very unusual, calming and atmospheric garden which carries many echoes of its past life as a country railway station.

TEA

Possibly one of the smallest and quirkiest cafés in the land, the Leaning Shed beside the station is a little self-service addition to the garden where visitors can help themselves to good coffee, home bakes and delectable organic ice cream Tue to Sun May to Aug. There are plenty of corners around the garden in which to sit and relax with these refreshments on a summers day. At weekends throughout the open season, additional tea, coffee and home-made cake is served to visitors inside The Garden Station where works of art and gardening books can also be enjoyed.

Harlow Carr

RHS Garden Harlow Carr, Crag Lane, Beckwithshaw, Harrogate HG3 1QB
Tel 01423 565418   www.rhs.org.uk/gardens/harlowcarr

Off B6162 (Otley Road), 1 1/2 miles from Harrogate centre

Open daily except Christmas day, 9.30–6 (or dusk if earlier)
Admission charge. Wheelchair access
Gift shop; plant centre
Owner Royal Horticultural Society

THE HERB GARDEN

Wonderful, varied gardens incorporating woods, a spectacular streamside garden, ornamental gardens and the Queen's Meadow which includes the Marie Curie Cancer Care Daffodil Garden, planted in 1997 with over 40,000 bulbs. A central purpose of the garden is to assess the suitability of plants for growing in northern climates. In the Winter Garden you will find varieties of hamamelis, mahonia, viburnum and pulmonaria, all of which are or have been, used medicinally. The Herb Garden, recently developed on heavy clay with additional drainage and grit, consists of eight beds, themed according to the way herbs are used. There are two beds each of culinary, cosmetic, medicinal and decorative herbs edged with *Lavandula* 'Hidcote' and *L.* 'Hidcote Pink'. Stone paths lead to the conservatory from where there are fine views through the garden. At the centre a sundial or birdbath will be embellished with thymes. Across the stream from the Queen's Meadow is South Field housing the National Collection of Rheum (rhubarb), known for its medicinal, culinary and decorative uses and first grown in 2,700 BC. The powdered root was brought via the Silk Route up until the sixteenth century. The Scented Garden, planted in 1995 has annual, perennial and shrubby plants and climbers, including roses, jasmine, honeysuckle, wisteria, *Syringa vulgaris* and many more. The Shrub Rose Border, underplanted with nepeta, is full of colour and fragrance in summer.

TEA

The Garden Rooms café, bar and restaurant, now run by Betty's, the famous Harrogate tea shop, offers afternoon teas, home-made cakes, cream teas and lunches. There is also a Garden Kiosk for humbler refreshments.

Herterton House Gardens and Nursery

Hartington, Cambo, Northumberland NE61 6BN
Tel 01670 774278

2 miles N of Cambo on the B6342

Open Apr to Sep daily except Tue and Thur 1.30–5.30.
Admission charge to gardens. Because of steep slopes not
suitable for wheelchairs
Nursery
Owner Frank and Marjorie Lawley

THE HERB GARDEN

The 1 acre of formal gardens with fine vernacular
stone walls is a delight and has some unusual
species. It began as a farmyard and has taken 27
years to complete. The design is based along the lines
of *A Country Housewife's Garden* by William
Lawson (1617), adapted to make a small twentieth-
century garden. Work is still proceeding. There are
formal hedges and topiaries in green and gold.

The Physic Garden centres round a silver pear
surrounded by beds of economic plants edged in
London pride or thrift. In 2001 a new Fancy Garden
was added with a parterre, terrace and gazebo in
which there is an exhibition of photographs showing
the garden's early construction. The nursery has a
selection of open-ground herbaceous plants from the
garden collection.

TEA

There are no teas at the garden but about 12 miles
away in Morpeth, the Chantry Tea Room, 9 Chantry
Place (Tel 01670 514414) offers a choice of teas and
cream teas, home-made cakes, cookies and puddings,
Or you could combine your Herterton visit with a
visit to Wallington (National Trust) which is only
three miles away, has fine herbaceous borders and a
restaurant serving teas.

Little Moreton Hall Herb Garden

Little Moreton Hall, Congleton, Cheshire CW12 4SD
Tel 01260 272 018

4 miles SW of Congleton, E of A34

Open end Mar to early Nov Wed to Sun and Bank Holiday
Mon 11.30–5; Nov to Dec Sat and Sun 11.30–4
Admission charge (free to NT members). Recommended
route for wheelchairs.
NT shop; herb plant sales
Owners The National Trust

Britain's most famous and arguably finest timber-
framed manor house was built in 1480 and owned by
the Moreton family for over 600 years. It is
surrounded by an unusual square moat.

THE HERB GARDEN

One section, planned as a knot garden by Paul Miles
and planted in 1975, was taken from a design from
Leonard Meager's *The Complete English Gardener*
published in 1670. It is in the form of an open knot
with gravel filling the spaces between the box edging.
Elizabethan herbs grown here include thrift, London
pride, wall germander, peony, marjoram, hyssop and
chamomile. Lavender is trained on short standards
as it would have been in Elizabethan days. Plants are
well labelled.

TEA

There is a licensed restaurant serving teas with
home-made cakes and scones.

Ness Botanic Gardens

The University of Liverpool Environmental and Horticultural
Research Station, Ness, Neston, Cheshire CH64 4AY
Tel 0151 3530123   www.nessgardens.org.uk

Between Neston and Burton off A540

Open daily except Christmas day Mar to Oct 9.30–5; Nov
to Feb 9.30–4

Admission charge Wheelchair access
Visitor centre, gift shop, plant sales
Owner University of Liverpool

Ness Botanic Gardens were created by Liverpool cotton merchant Arthur Kilpin Bulley in 1898. In 1948 it was presented to the University of Liverpool and now consists of gardens, greenhouses and experimental grounds – in all 25 hectares of superb botanic garden overlooking the Dee Estuary. Notable collections include Himalayan and Chinese rhododendrons and azaleas, heathers, roses, specimen trees and herbs. There is a short avenue of limes, a rose garden, a rock garden, a woodland garden, a water garden and an arboretum. Be wary, the gardens are undulating and the paths can become slippery.

THE HERB GARDEN

The Ledsham herb garden was laid out in the spring of 1974 on the site originally levelled for tennis courts. The famous laburnum arch is part of the Ledsham garden, where traditional culinary and medicinal herbs grow alongside lavender, *Artemisia abrotanum* ('old man') which used to be strewn on floors to be crushed underfoot and exude its scent. The garden provides examples of families like the umbellifers (parsley, fennel and coriander for example), flowering and non-flowering clones, monocotyledons and dicotyledons and it is therefore a useful teaching area.

TEA

There is a licensed refreshment room which provides teas as well as light lunches.

Norton Priory Walled Garden

Norton Priory Museum and Walled Garden, Tudor Road, Manor Park, Runcorn, Cheshire WA7 1SX
Tel 01928 569895   www.nortonpriory.org

2 miles E of Runcorn, 3 miles from Junction 11 of M56
Open daily 12-4 (5 in summer, 6 on busy weekends)
Shop; plant sales
Owner Norton Priory Museum Trust

This peaceful 38 acres of woodland gardens contains the twelfth-century ruins of an Augustinian priory. The walled garden belonged to a Georgian house which became derelict in 1921. There is a fruit garden and herbaceous borders first laid out in the 1760s and lots of alleyways and arbours.

THE HERB GARDEN

The reconstructed medieval herb garden was created in 2003 with the help of volunteers from Astmoor Day Services, a day centre for adults with learning disabilities. It is said to be 'as authentic a copy of a monastic herb garden as it is possible to have' with raised narrow rectangular beds which are easy to reach for cultivating and harvesting. Norton Priory has many old roses, medlars, apples, pears and holds the National Collection of Quince (*Cydonia oblonga*).

TEA

A pleasant coffee shop offers teas as well.

Ripley Castle

Ripley, Harrogate, N Yorks HG3 3AY
Tel 01423 770152   www.ripleycastle.co.uk

3¹/₂ miles N of Harrogate off the A61 between Harrogate and Ripon. Short walk through Market Square from car park in village

Open all year, gardens every day Jul to Aug 9–5.30; other months Tue, Thur, Fri, Easter and May bank holidays. Please phone first as opening times may vary
Admission charge. Wheelchair access (electric mobility buggy available)
Gift shop; outdoor sales of herbs, flowers and plants
Owner The Ingilby family

The Ingilbys have owned this historic and much altered castle for seven centuries and still live there today. You can have an entertaining guided tour of the house or you can choose to visit the park, grounds and gardens on their own. As well as an impressive collection of tropical plants in the hot houses, the pleasure grounds contain a collection of specimen trees and there are thousands of spring bulbs, a park walk with an ornamental lake and fallow deer grazing under thousand-year-old oak trees.

THE HERB GARDEN

The 5 acres of walled gardens are the home of the National Hyacinth Collection and in late April or early May you can see rows of 40–60 varieties in bloom. The scent is spectacular. This garden also holds an extensive and magnificent culinary herb bed and the Bell Gate leads to the kitchen garden in which is grown an extraordinary collection of old and rare varieties of vegetables grown in co-operation with the Henry Doubleday Research Association.

TEA

The Castle Tearooms, across the road from the Gift Shop, has picnic tables for sunny days and offers cups of tea, coffee and hot chocolate as well as freshly baked scones, cakes, biscuits and cream teas.

The William Turner Garden

Carlisle Park, Off Castle Square, Morpeth, Northumberland, NE61 1YD   Tel 01670 500777
email: carlislepark@castlemorpeth.gov.uk

There is no parking in Carlisle Park but metered parking is available throughout Morpeth

Open daily, 8–dusk.
Admission free. Wheelchair access.
Owner Castle Morpeth Borough Council

THE HERB GARDEN

A contemporary interpretation of a Tudor physic and knot garden, the William Turner Garden contains examples of plants used in sixteenth-century herbal medicine and featured in Turner's *A New Herball*, published in three parts from 1551 to 1568. The garden is a tribute to Turner (the 'father of English botany') who was born in Morpeth in 1508. It was created as a direct response to requests from Morpeth residents to provide a botanic garden celebrating his life. It contains only plants that would have been found in his lifetime and reflects the forms and features of a renaissance garden of its time. It is divided into three components: the Physic Garden on a lower terrace, a Medieval Garden on an upper terrace, and a Botanic Garden on the connecting ramp between these two terraces. The garden is reached from the formal gardens in Carlisle Park, known for their annual bedding and carpet bedding displays, or down some steps from the bottom of Ha Hill, an eleventh-century motte.

TEA

The closest tea room with very good scones, is the Chantry Tea Rooms on Chantry Place. There are numerous other tea rooms, coffee shops and public houses within easy walking distance of Carlisle Park and the William Turner Garden.

York Gate Herb Garden

York Gate, Back Church Lane, Adel, Leeds LS16 8DW
Tel 01132 678240   www.perennial.org.uk

2¹/₂ miles SE of Bramhope just off A6600

Open Apr to Sep Thur, Sun, Bank Holiday Mon 2–5; every Thur evening in Jul 6.30–9
Admission charge. Limited wheelchair access
Plants for sale
Owner Perennial Gardeners' Royal Benevolent Society

This garden was created by the Spencer family between 1951 and 1994. In 1982 Robin Spencer died suddenly at the age of 48. For the next 12 years it was nurtured by his mother Sybil, a gifted plantswoman. In just 1 acre of ground the Spencers created a diverse plant collection which remains today and includes a nut walk, peony bed, iris border, white and silver garden, pavement maze, miniature pinetum, an espaliered cedar and an unusual herb garden. The charity will continue to maintain the garden in sympathy with the Spencers' design and with Sybil's wish to attract visitors for education and pleasure.

THE HERB GARDEN

The herb garden is formal in design and the plants are grown for decoration rather than for use. It measures only 9m x 3m and is an enclosed leafy walkway backed by high yew hedges. The basic symmetry is accentuated by a central pathway leading to a classical summerhouse complete with columns. On each side of the path the borders contain herbs such as sage, giant alliums, bronze fennel, angelica and balm interspersed with clipped box globes and spirals to give a green framework during winter. The garden is full of small touches to surprise and enchant from unusual little containers of aromatic herbs to Japanese stone lanterns among clipped box shapes.

TEA

Tea, coffee and biscuits are available from June to end Sep. For something a little more substantial, Wildings Tea Room and Riverside Terrace, Nidd Walk, Pately Bridge (about 8 miles N of the garden on the B6265) is in a beautiful setting overlooking the River Nidd. This traditional tea room serves teas including Earl Grey and Yorkshire in china pots plus ginger scones and tea bread. Open Jul to mid-Oct Tue to Sun 10.30–4.30, Wed and Thur 10.30–4.30 and bank holidays. Tel 01423 711152.

Yorkshire Garden World

Main Road, West Haddlesey, Nr Selby, N Yorkshire YO8 8QA
Tel 01757 228 279   www.yorkshiregardenw.f9.co.uk

A short way off the A19 at Chapel Haddlesey

Open daily 9.30–5.30, Sun and bank holidays 10–5; closed Mon
Small admission charge for gardens. Wheelchair access
Shop (herbal remedies, gifts etc.); comprehensive nursery; lectures, courses herb dinners
Owner Carole Atkinson

The gardens were started in 1984 in a 4-acre field and now include water gardens, a pygmy pinetum, a winter garden, perennials and several herb gardens.

THE HERB GARDEN

There is information on the history and uses of herbs, all set within a wild garden of meadow and woodland flowers.

The Knot Garden is laid out as a seventeenth-century garden. The Lovers' Garden is full of plants which were given as secret messages. The Open Air Herb Museum is an acre of squares set in grass, each square with a separate herb. The Aromatherapy Garden grows the hardy herbs used for distilling and producing essential oils. Culpeper's Zodiac Garden is in the shape of a wheel depicting the star signs. The Santolina and Rose Garden holds the National Collection of Santolinas and the National Collection of Highly Scented Roses. Everything is organically grown. This is a good garden to spend some time in. There is plenty to intrigue people of all ages and interests.

TEA

There is a large tearoom with a pergola serving Taylor's teas and home-made food, including freshly made sandwiches.

WALES

Penlan
Uchaf

National Botanic Garden of Wales

FISHGUARD

Aberglasney Gardens

CARMARTHEN

SWANSEA

CARDIFF

Dyffryn Gardens

The sites of the gardens shown on
this map are approximate. They will give
an indication as to how you might plan
your visits. For precise instructions on
finding the gardens, please refer to the
specific information for each garden.

Aberglasney Gardens

Llangathen, Carmarthenshire SA32 8QH
Tel 01558 668998   www.aberglasney.org.uk

*Just off the A40 at Broad Oak, 4 miles W of Llandeilo and
12 miles E of Carmarthen*

Open daily summer 10–6; winter 10.30–4
Admission charge. Wheelchair access to much of the
garden
Shop; plant sales; illustrated guide book
Owner Aberglasney Garden Trust

Aberglasney House is part medieval with later
additions and some of the enormous walls date from
the sixteenth century. The centuries' old garden was
discovered in the 1990s by William Rankin (who was
also the prime mover in establishing the National
Botanic Garden of Wales), covered by a jungle of
undergrowth and full of Japanese knotweed. Its
restoration has been sponsored by an American
benefactor, Frank Cabot. Since 1999 it has been run
as a private charitable trust. There are woodland
walks holding many rare plants including ferns,
rhododendrons and magnolias. An ambitious project
is now underway to cover the derelict part of the
house with an atrium and turn the rooms beneath
into separate indoor 'gardens' housing exotic plants.

THE HERB GARDEN

The present garden consists of several separate
spaces including a herbaceous garden designed by
Penelope Hobhouse, a walled kitchen garden, an
ancient fish pond and a raised parapet walkway
allowing bird's eye views of parts of the garden. The
Cloister Garden is the oldest part of the garden and
the most protected with its sixteenth-century arched
stone walls. Its centre is a broderie parterre of grass
interplanted with spring bulbs that would have been
grown in the sixteenth century. This is surrounded
by lead containers holding two species of orange
trees – bitter and sweet – also from the 1500s. These

go into the glasshouse in winter and are replaced by clipped box balls. There are flourishing lavender beds and soapwort in odd corners. The walled kitchen garden grows decorative vegetables and culinary herbs, all organic, that are used in the attractive café.

TEA

The café is on a raised area giving a view of a box parterre filled with herbs and the fish pond with its centre of bulrushes. You can watch the chef make his way to the vegetable garden to collect herbs for your tea. Teas, herb teas and home-made cakes and scones are available as well as light lunches.

Dyffryn Botanic Garden

St Nicholas, Vale of Glamorgan, CF5 6SU
Tel 0129 2059 3328   www.dyffryngardens.org.uk

10 minutes south of Cardiff, signposted from the A4232

Open Apr to Sep 10–6; Oct 10–5; Nov to Mar 10–4
Admission charge. Wheelchair accessibility for some of gardens
Shop; plant sales; garden plan but no guide book
Owner Vale of Glamorgan County Council

The present stately house was built in 1893 and Thomas Mawson, a well-known landscape architect, was commissioned to design a garden to complement it. In true Victorian manner, intended to reflect the travels and interests of its owner, it consists of a 'collection' of different garden styles including a Pompeiian garden, a theatre garden, a very long double herbaceous border, a medieval garden all divided by and given structure with clipped box and yew. There's an enormous lawn with a central canal, woodland walks, a number of rare and interesting trees, a rose garden, a vine walk (due to be restored) and a forest of clipped yew umbrellas. Little rills of water enliven the environment everywhere.

THE HERB GARDEN

Among the collection of enclosed gardens is the Apothecaries' Garden. This is not laid out in the usual formal beds but as a winding walk offering a good collection of medicinal herbs grown under and around taller trees. For example wall germander is used to make a low circular hedge round an enormous pittosporum and round every corner is a new surprise and a new scent to identify and enjoy.

TEA

A circular modern wooden building with an outlook over the front of the house through glass windows provides a pleasant place to take a cup of tea or coffee. Herbal teas are available with some interesting cakes including Welsh specialities. Closed from November to March.

National Botanic Garden of Wales

Llanarthne, Carmarthenshire, SA32 8HG
Tel 01558 667148/9   www.gardenofwales.org.uk

Just off the A48 which links to the M4 and M5 – about an hour's drive from Cardiff

Open daily except Christmas Day; Apr to Oct 10–6; Nov to Mar 10–4.30
Admission charge. Wheelchair access
Shop; plant sales
Owner National Botanic Garden of Wales Trust

The NBGW was opened in 2000 on the eighteenth-century estate of Middleton, which once belonged to William Paxton (no relation to Paxton of the Crystal Palace). Paxton's Tower (now owned by the National Trust) overlooks the garden from a nearby hill and his spectacular water features are to be restored. Free tours are available.

THE HERB GARDENS

Like most botanic gardens, the NBGW is really one
great herb garden. Inside the Great Glasshouse (the
world's largest single span greenhouse designed by
Norman Foster) are plants from California, the
Mediterranean basin, Chile, South Africa and
Australia, growing among rock faces, ravines,
streams, waterfalls and lakes landscaped by Kathryn
Gusstavson. The biomass furnace maintains the heat
at an even temperature. Rainwater is collected in two
vast tanks for irrigation. The central theme of the
garden is to 'show how plants are the life sustainers
on whose potential and diversity the future of
mankind depends'. The many features and interests
of this garden make it well worth spending a day
here: there are the endangered plants from Wales.
The Wallace Garden is named after Welshman Alfred
Wallace who contributed to the theory of evolution.
Its paths are laid out in the double helix of DNA and
its beds show plants that have been selectively bred
or have gone through spontaneous mutation. The
eighteenth-century walled garden, now largely
restored, has a double wall providing a microclimate
enabling the growing season for fruits to be extended
by up to three months.

The Apothecaries' Garden holds a wide variety of
medicinal herbs. It is terraced up a hillside and
attractively mulched with local slate chippings. This
keeps down weeds and helps retain water while
looking highly attractive. Nearby is a nursery bed
where endangered local plants are being nurtured
prior to being returned to the wild. There are also
lakes and wildflower meadows.

TEA

The courtyard café provides tea and cakes as well as
light lunches in a sheltered environment with tables
indoors or out.

Penlan Uchaf

Penlan Uchaf Farm Gardens, Gwaun Valley, Fishguard,
Pembrokeshire SA65 9UA
Tel 01348 881388

*7 miles SE of Fishguard. Take B4313 Narbeth Road and
carry on until you see the brown tourist sign*

Open Mar to Nov 9–5. Opening times and charges may
alter, please telephone first
Admission charge. Wheelchair access to most of the
garden
Owner Mr and Mrs Vaughan

THE HERB GARDENS

Penlan Uchaf consists of 3 acres of gardens, of which
1 acre consists of herbs and wild flowers, in
landscaped surroundings at the top of a steep and
beautiful valley with stunning views with a fast
flowing stream. The garden has a sensory area for
the blind and disabled with a raised garden
containing more than 100 different varieties of herbs
and wild flowers. Mr and Mrs Vaughan are still
developing the garden with the intention of
providing colours in all seasons. There is a 27m
pergola sensationally covered with sweet peas.

TEA

There is a tea room from which you get a choice of
teas including herbal teas as well as cream teas or
soup and a roll if required, and a fantastic view over
the Preseli Hills.

SCOTLAND

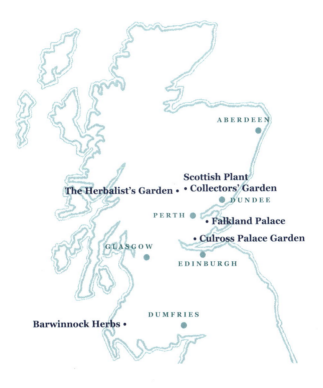

The sites of the gardens shown on this map are approximate. They will give an indication as to how you might plan your visits. For precise instructions on finding the gardens, please refer to the specific information for each garden.

Barwinnock Herbs

Barrhill, Ayrshire, KA26 0RB
Tel 01465 821 338   www.barwinnock.com

Off the B7027 between Newton Stewart and Barrhill

Open Apr to end Oct 10–6
Admission free. Limited wheelchair access
Owner Dave and Mon Holtom

Barwinnock Nursery is based at a small stone-built
cottage in the remote and windswept south-west
Scottish moorland. All except the most frost sensitive
varieties are grown outside in the cool climate. The
nursery makes its own organic compost and no
chemical fertilisers or pesticides are used. The plants
achieve a well developed root system and become
capable of resisting the effects of weather and insect
attack. When planted out they soon become
established and quickly develop.

THE HERB GARDEN

Barwinnock is probably the most remote and
exposed herb garden you are likely to visit. It is open
to all the westerly gales and storms of a south-west
Scottish winter. The willow, *Salix viminalis*, which
can be used for coarse basketwork is the only wind-
break. This is a herb garden to walk into, to enjoy the
fragrance of the plants and harvest them for use.
Within the garden you can walk into the beds,
through small paths and along stepping stones to
discover what might be growing. Larger plants have
to be peered round to find others. Paths and borders
often merge. There are shrubs overhanging and
plants underfoot so that you really feel part of the
garden rather than just looking at it from afar.

Emphasis is on placing plants in the conditions
they prefer so they may thrive naturally. A scree
slope and raised beds are used for alpines and plants
that prefer dry conditions, while the shady, lower
ground has the damp loving varieties. In the spirit of
herbs growing naturally and with the minimum of

imposition from the owners, regular geometric shapes have been avoided. Seed heads are left so that plants can self-sow.

TEA

Tea is not provided at Barwinnock but Wigtown has several cafés to choose from including: Café Rendezvous, 2 Agnew Crescent, Wigtown, Newton Stewart (01988 402074); The Reading Lasses Café, South Main Street, Wigtown (01988 402391).

Culross Palace Garden

Culross Palace, Culross, Fife KY12 8JH
Tel 01383 880359   www.nts.org.uk

Off the A985, 12 miles W of the Forth Road Bridge and 4 miles E of Kincardine Bridge

Open in conjunction with Culross Palace: Apr to Sep and weekends in Oct
Admission charge. Wheelchair access
Gift shop; herbs for sale
Owner National Trust for Scotland

The Palace is a late sixteenth/early seventeenth-century house built by a wealthy merchant.

THE HERB GARDEN

The garden, a model of a seventeenth-century garden, reflects what such a merchant of the period might have grown to support his household. It is terraced on a steep slope and mainly consists of raised beds. It is partitioned by willow hurdle fences and furnished with paths of crushed shells. There are vegetables, culinary and medicinal herbs, soft fruit and flowering meads. This garden contains a wealth of now scarce herbs and perennials that would have been grown around 1600.

TEA

There is a tearoom in Bessie Bar Hall where you can get a cup of tea with cakes and biscuits.

Falkland Palace, Garden and Old Burgh

Falkland, Cupar, Fife KY15 7BU
Tel 01337 857 397   www.nts.org.uk

On the A912 10 miles from M90 Junction 8; 11 miles N of Kirkcaldy

Open Mar to Oct, Mon to Sat 10–6, Sun 1–5
Admission charge. Wheelchair access
Shop, plant sales, publications
Owner National Trust for Scotland

Falkland Palace, set in the conservation village of Falkland, has been a place of kings ever since the days of the Stuarts. Kings and queens hunted wild boar and deer in the forest and Mary Queen of Scots was fond of it. Here is the original Royal Tennis Court (1539), the oldest still in use in Britain.

The large and lovely garden has well maintained lawns, mature trees and colourful planting.

THE HERB GARDEN

The herb garden border is small but fascinating and features plants and quotations from John Gerard's *Herball* published in 1597. A garden designed by Percy Crane in 1947–52 has three herbaceous borders enclosing a wide lawn with a variety of shrubs and trees.

TEA

You can't get tea at the Palace unless you are organising a wedding or event, but The Hayloft (Tel 01337 857590) tucked away in Back Wynd, Falkland serves a wide selection of home-made cakes and scones, a selection of teas including green tea, and vegetarian meals; Kind Kittock's Kitchen, Cross Wynd, Falkland (Tel 01337 857477) serves speciality teas, loose leaf teas, Russian tea with lemon, and cream teas, all with home-made scones and cakes, baked daily.

The Herbalist's Garden

Garden Cottage, Pitnacree, Strathtay, Perthshire PH9 OLW
Tel 01887 840773

Pitnacree is 4 miles from Ballinluig, just off the A827.

Open May to Oct Tue to Thur and Sat or by arrangement
Admission free; donations welcome. Wheelchair access
Plants for sale.
Owner Jacqui Hazzard

THE HERB GARDEN

The garden has been designed with many factors in
mind. It is a working garden for the herbalist Jacqui
Hazzard; it is a demonstration of the methods of
permaculture and it incorporates features to allow
people with physical disabilities both to access the
garden and to work in it. Medicinal herbs are
cultivated for the dispensary, culinary herbs, food
crops and fruit for the table.

TEA

Teas are not available at the garden but The Pantry
Tearoom, 25a Dunkeld Street (A827) serves teas,
coffees and various home-baked light snacks
(Tel 01887 829722).

Scottish Plant Collectors' Garden

Pitlochry Festival Theatre, Pitlochry, Perthshire PH16 5DR
Tel 01796 484600   www.explorersgarden.com

*On entering Pitlochry from the A9 follow signs for Pitlochry
Festival Theatre. The garden is on the hillside between the
Theatre and the famous Fish Ladder*

Open 24 Mar to 31 Oct Mon to Sat 10–5 Sun 11–5.
Admission free; charge for guided tours. Wheelchair access
Small gift shop; plants for sale
Owner Pitlochry Festival Theatre

139

THE HERB GARDEN

Scotland has produced some of the world's most successful plant collectors. This garden, created in conjunction with the Royal Botanic garden Edinburgh, is a celebration of their fascinating lives and the amazing numbers of plants they brought back from far lands. Among them are David Douglas (1798–c1834) who explored in USA, Hawaii, Portugal and the Galapagos Islands and introduced the Douglas Fir (*Pseudotsuga menziesii*) and flowering currant (*Ribes sanguineum*) among many other plants that changed our landscape. George Forrest (1837–1932) brought back 30,000 seeds and over 10,000 plants from China, Tibet and Burma. His finds included species of iris, primula, camellia, jasmine and orchids although he is mainly remembered for the numerous rhododendrons he brought back. The garden is separated into geographical sections to show where plants originated so you can imagine yourself in a North American glade, move on through Nepal, to South Africa, China and Japan. At the entrance to the garden The Heart of Scotland Herb Society has planted and maintains an area of herbs including pulmonarias, dwarf and variegated comfrey, house leeks, southernwood, sweet woodruff and selfheal. Here visitors can rest and enjoy the wonderful view over the river.

TEA

Teas, bar facilities and full meals are available in the restaurant within the theatre building.

Specialist Herb Farms & Nurseries

Arne Herbs
Limeburn Nurseries, Chew Magna, Bristol BS40 8QW.
Tel 01275 333399; Fax 01275 333399
www.arneherbs.co.uk

Bernwode Plants
Kingswood Lane, Ludgershall,
Bucks HP18 9RB
Tel 01844 237415
www.bernwodeplants.co.uk

Blackbrook Herb Gardens
Blackbrook Cottage, Alderley Road, Wilmslow,
Cheshire SK9 1PZ
Tel 01625 539166

Bodmin Plant and Herb Nursery
Laveddon Mill, Laninval Hill, Bodmin,
Cornwall PL30 5JU
Tel 01208 72837; Fax 01208 76491

The Botanic Nursery
Bath Road, Arworth,
Nr Melksham, Wiltshire SN12 8NU
Tel m. 07850 328756; Fax 01225 700953
www.thebotanicnursery.com

Brogdale Horticultural Trust
Brogdale Road, Faversham, Kent ME13 8XZ
Tel 01795 535286
www.brogdale.org

Candlesby Herbs
Cross Keys Cottage,
Candlesby, Spilsby, Lincs PE23 5SF
Tel 01754 890 211
www.candlesbyherbs.co.uk

The Citrus Centre
West Mare Lane,
Pulborough, West Sussex RH20 2EA
Tel 01798 872786
www.citruscentre.co.uk

The Cottage Herbery

Mill House,
Boraston, Nr Tenbury Wells, Worcs
WR15 8LZ
Tel 01584 781575; Fax 01584 781483
www.thecottageherbery.co.uk

Dysons Nurseries (specialise salvias),

At Great Comp Garden, Comp Lane,
Platt, Nr Sevenoaks, Kent TN15 8QS
Tel 01732 886154
www.greatcomp.co.uk/dysons-nurseries.htm

Edulis

1 Flowers Place, Ashampstead,
Berkshire RG8 8SG
Tel 01635 578113; Fax 01635 578113
www.edulis.co.uk

Elsworth Herbs (National Collection of Artemisia)

Avenue Farm Cottage, 31 Smith Street, Elsworth,
Cambridge CB3 8HY
Tel 01954 267414

Global Orange Groves UK

Horton Road, Horton Heath, Wimborne,
Dorset BH21 7JN
Tel 01202 826 244
www.globalorangegroves.co.uk

The Herb Garden & Historical Plant Nursery

Pentre Berw, Gaerwen, Anglesey,
Wales LL60 6LF
Tel 01248 422 208
www.HistoricalPlants.co.uk
(Mail order only)

Herbs at Myddfai

Beiliglas, Myddfai, Nr Llandovery,
Carmarthenshire, Wales SA20 0QB
Tel 01550 720494
www.myddfai.com

Highdown Nursery

New Hall Lane, Small Dole, Nr Henfield,
West Sussex BN5 9YH
Tel 01273 492976; Fax 01273 492976

Jekkas Herb Farm
Rose Cottage, Shellards Lane, Alveston,
Bristol, Avon BS35 3SY
Tel 01454 418878; Fax 01454 411988
www.jekkasherbfarm.com

John Chambers (herbs and wild flowers seeds)
15 Westleigh Road, Burton Seagrave, Kettering,
Northants NN15 5AJ
Tel 01933 652562

Langley Boxwood Nursery
Rake, Nr Liss , Hants GU33 7JL
Tel 01730 894467
www.boxwood.co.uk

LW Plants
23 Wroxham Way, Harpenden, Herts AL5 4PP
Tel 01582 768467
www.thymus.co.uk

Norfolk Herbs
Blackberry Farm, Dillington, Nr Gressenhall
Dereham, Norfolk NR19 2QD
Tel 01362 860812; Fax 01362 860812
www.norfolkherbs.co.uk

Oak Cottage Herbs
Oak House, Astley, Shrewsbury, Shropshire SY4 4BP
Tel 01939 210219; Fax 01939 210219

Reads Nursery (citrus)
Hales Hall, Loddon, Norfolk NR14 6QW
Tel 01508 548395
www.readsnursery.co.uk

Period Plants
24 Hamstead Marshall, Newbury, Berkshire
RG20 0HR
Tel 01488 657248
www.arcadian-archives.com/periodplants.htm

Poyntzfield Herb Nursery
Black Isle, By Dingwall, Cromarty,
Scotland IV7 8LX
Tel 01381 610352
www.poyntzfieldherbs.co.uk

St Kitts Herbery

Starapark, Camelford, Cornwall PL32 9XH.

Tel 01840 213442

www.stkittsherbery.co.uk

Salley Gardens

32 Lansdowne Drive, West Bridgford

Nottingham NG2 7FJ

Tel 0115 9233878

Southview Nurseries (specialises pinks)

Chequers Lane, Eversley Cross, Hook,

Hampshire RG27 ONT

Tel 0118 9732206

www.southviewnurseries.co.uk

Stonecrop Herbs

East Lound, Haxey. Doncaster, S Yorkshire DN9 2LR

Tel 01427 753355; Fax 01427 753355

Suffolk Herbs

Monks Farm, Coggeshall Road, Kelvedon

Essex CO5 9PG

Tel 01376 572456; Fax 01376 571189

www.suffolkherbs.com

Trent Cottage Herbs

Trent Nurseries, Tittensor Road, Tittensor,

Stoke-on-Trent ST12 9HG

Tel 01782 372395

www.trentcottageherbs.co.uk

Wye Valley Plants

The Nurtons, Tintern, Gwent NP6 7NX

Tel/fax 01291 689253

Yorkshire Lavender

The Yorkshire Lavender Farm, Terrington, York

North Yorkshire YO60 6QB

Tel 01653 648430; Fax 01653 648008

www.lavenderland.co.uk